Kahoud and Knafo explore the connection between sexuality, substance abuse, and creativity through a psychoanalytic lens, and they bring a fresh nuanced perspective that will inform psychodynamic practitioners as well as sophisticated readers. They elucidate the secret agendas behind sexuality and reach beyond behavior into a magical mystery tour of inner psychic experience. The case examples humanize the most extreme attempts to use sex as reparation for life's universal harshness and inevitable losses.

Suzanne Iasenza, Sex Therapist and Co-Editor,
Lesbians, Feminism and Psychoanalysis

The existentialists have proposed that the lot for us humans is one of infinite thirst juxtaposed to essential limitation. Kahoud and Knafo understand this well. They trace the vicissitudes of this aspect of our human nature to earliest phases of childhood development. The authors stress the importance of omnipotent fantasies and attitudes as defenses against a sense of impermanence and powerlessness. The book is well written and clear, free of obscuring jargon, and offers critically important psychodynamic understanding to explain how sex, drugs and creativity can become such a compelling force in the lives of susceptible individuals.

Edward J. Khantzian, MD, Professor of Psychiatry, Harvard Medical
School, Author, *Treating Addiction as a Human Process*

This book is a tour de force! With delicious writing, it explores the relationships among early trauma, existential dread, omnipotent fantasy, and sexuality, drugs, and creativity. The reader learns how omnipotent fantasy is expressed in perversion, addiction, and creativity and how particular responses to our existential dilemmas can transform self-defeating behavior into positive, creative activity. Kahoud and Knafo led me to reflect deeply on how these dynamics operate within me and are relevant to my work with patients. I highly recommend this book.

Andrew Tatarsky, PhD; Author, *Harm Reduction Psychotherapy:*
A New Treatment for Drug and Alcohol Problems

Sex, Drugs, and Creativity

In *Sex, Drugs, and Creativity: Searching for Magic in a Disenchanted World*, Kahoud and Knafo take a close look at omnipotent fantasies in three domains: sex, drugs, and creativity. They demonstrate how these fantasies emerge and how artists draw on them both to create and destroy – sometimes simultaneously – and how understanding this can help psychoanalysts work more effectively with these individuals.

Using the personal statements of influential artists and entertainers, in addition to clinical material, the authors examine the omnipotence of self-destruction as it contends with that of creative artists. The authors argue that creative artists use omnipotent fantasies to imagine the world differently – this enables them to produce their art, but also leaves these artists vulnerable to addiction. Chapters devoted to Stephen King and Anne Sexton demonstrate the ways these authors used drugs and alcohol to fuel imagination and inspire creative output while simultaneously doing harm to themselves. A detailed case study also demonstrates successful clinical work with a creative substance user.

Sex, Drugs, and Creativity will appeal to anyone interested in the links between creativity and substance use, and will be of great use to psychoanalysts and mental health practitioners working with these challenging clients.

Dustin Kahoud is a clinical psychologist with specialized training in the treatment of addictions. He has received postgraduate training in psychoanalysis and psychotherapy as a candidate at the Derner Institute, where he also teaches classes on addictions to psychology graduate students. Dustin Kahoud continues to write about the omnipotent fantasies that drive human behavior, and he maintains a private practice in Great Neck, NY.

Danielle Knafo is a clinical psychologist and psychoanalyst. She is a professor at Long Island University and New York University. She has written and lectured extensively on the subjects of trauma, creativity, and sexuality. Her most recent book (with Routledge) is *The Age of Perversion: Desire and Technology in Psychoanalysis and Culture.*

Psychological Issues

Series Editor: David Wolitzky

The basic mission of *Psychological Issues* is to contribute to the further development of psychoanalysis as a science, as a respected scholarly enterprise, as a theory of human behavior, and as a therapeutic method.

Over the past 50 years, the series has focused on fundamental aspects and foundations of psychoanalytic theory and clinical practice, as well as on work in related disciplines relevant to psychoanalysis. *Psychological Issues* does not aim to represent or promote a particular point of view. The contributions cover broad and integrative topics of vital interest to all psychoanalysts as well as to colleagues in related disciplines. They cut across particular schools of thought and tackle key issues, such as the philosophical underpinnings of psychoanalysis, psychoanalytic theories of motivation, conceptions of therapeutic action, the nature of unconscious mental functioning, psychoanalysis and social issues, and reports of original empirical research relevant to psychoanalysis. The authors often take a critical stance toward theories and offer a careful theoretical analysis and conceptual clarification of the complexities of theories and their clinical implications, drawing upon relevant empirical findings from psychoanalytic research as well as from research in related fields.

The Editorial Board continues to invite contributions from social/behavioral sciences such as anthropology and sociology, from biological sciences such as physiology and the various brain sciences, and from scholarly humanistic disciplines such as philosophy, law, and ethics. Volumes 1-64 in this series were published by International Universities Press. Volumes 65-69 were published by Jason Aronson.

Routledge titles in this series:

Vol. 78 Core Concepts in Contemporary Psychoanalysis: Clinical, Research Evidence and Conceptual Critiques *Morris N. Eagle*

Vol. 79 Psychoanalytic Thinking: A Dialectical Critique of Contemporary Theory and Practice *Donald L. Carveth*

Vol. 80 Sex, Drugs, and Creativity: Searching for Magic in a Disenchanted World *Dustin Kahoud and Danielle Knafo*

Sex, Drugs, and Creativity

Searching for Magic in a Disenchanted World

Dustin Kahoud and Danielle Knafo

Routledge
Taylor & Francis Group

LONDON AND NEW YORK

First published 2019
by Routledge
2 Park Square, Milton Park, Abingdon, Oxon OX14 4RN

and by Routledge
711 Third Avenue, New York, NY 10017

Routledge is an imprint of the Taylor & Francis Group, an informa business

British Library Cataloguing-in-Publication Data
A catalogue record for this book is available from the British Library

Library of Congress Cataloging-in-Publication Data
Names: Kahoud, Dustin, author. | Knafo, Danielle, author.
Title: Sex, drugs and creativity : searching for magic in a disenchanted world / Dustin Kahoud and Danielle Knafo.
Description: Abingdon, Oxon ; New York, NY : Routledge, 2018.
Identifiers: LCCN 2018008045 | ISBN 9781138956087 (hardback) |
ISBN 9781138956094 (pbk.) | ISBN 9781317353447 (epub) |
ISBN 9781317353430 (mobipocket)
Subjects: LCSH: Creative ability. | Compulsive behavior. | Personality and creative ability.
Classification: LCC BF408 .K578 2018 | DDC 153.3/5--dc23
LC record available at https://lccn.loc.gov/2018008045

ISBN: 978-1-138-95608-7 (hbk)
ISBN: 978-1-138-95609-4 (pbk)
ISBN: 978-1-315-66588-7 (ebk)

Typeset in Times New Roman
by Taylor & Francis Books

This book is dedicated to our ultimate creative efforts:

Roland and Josie (Dustin Kahoud),
and Gavriel (Danielle Knafo).

Contents

Acknowledgements

Dustin Kahoud

I would like to thank my coauthor Danielle Knafo, who was originally my professor and doctoral dissertation committee chair. Danielle's creative pursuits and generous mentorship have been an inspiration to me. She was first to propose undertaking this project as a theoretical dissertation and encouraged me to push the limits of traditional psychological inquiry even further. This book is the final product of that particular collaboration.

I am very thankful to my wife Alexis for proofreading and even listening to me read aloud parts of the book. Most important, I am grateful for her support while I pursued the solitary work of a writer, especially as a new father. With an infant in one arm and a toddler trailing alongside her, Alexis never lost patience with me as we completed the project. As for my children, I never knew the experience of being grateful for interruptions until it was in the form of Roland's and Josie's voices echoing through the ceiling.

The support and encouragement of my parents have made all the difference in my becoming a psychologist and writer; their unwavering confidence helped me pursue a career in which I can honestly say I love to come to work every day.

Finally, I thank my analysts and supervisors, and patients, past and present. While the work with some has ended and continues with others, they are all present with me each day as I work with my patients.

Danielle Knafo

It is not every day that a student takes my advice and develops his dissertation into a publishable manuscript. I am very proud of Dustin for taking on the challenge. I am also quite pleased to have been part of it. Sex, drugs, creativity, and unconscious fantasies are subjects that have intrigued me for quite some time. I am thrilled we could advance this topic further.

We thank David Wolitzky, our series editor, for his belief in this project and his valuable suggestions to early drafts of chapters. Rocco Lo Bosco also read an earlier version of the manuscript and made important recommendations.

We feel fortunate to have had the careful and wise editing of the manuscript by Maryellen Lo Bosco, editor extraordinaire. Abigail Frawley was extremely helpful in obtaining permissions for the quotations throughout the book, and Ro'ee Meyer and William Rung created the index. Thanks, too, to the wonderful Routledge staff – Kate Hawes, Charles Bath, Charlotte Taylor, Katherine Finn – who have helped to bring this book to final fruition. We are grateful to artist Giancarlo Biagi for his beautiful illustration of Icarus on our book jacket.

Finally, we thank our patients who gave permission to write about them and who are our greatest teachers.

We are grateful to the following for allowing quotations from their works:

Bryan Birchmeier at University of Michigan Press for the following titles: Anne Sexton: Telling the tale (copyright 1988, University of Michigan Press) and No Evil Star: Selected essays, interviews, and prose (copyright 1985, University of Michigan Press)
HarperCollins Publishers for epigraph from Sylvia Plath's The Bell Jar (copyright 1971 by Harper & Row)
Ebony Lane at MacMillan for Rogak's The Haunted Heart (copyright 2008, Thomas Dunne Books)
Yessenia Santos at Simon and Schuster for Stephen King's On writing: A memoir of the craft (copyright 2000 by Scriber) and Danse Macabre (copyright 1981 by Gallery Books)
Professor Roberto Magiera Unger for lines from The self awakened: Pragmatism unbound (copyright 2007, Harvard University Press)
Sam Moore at Penguin Random House for Stephen King's The Shining (copyright 1977, Penguin Group)
Ron Hussey and Isabelle Prince at Houghton Mifflin Harcourt for excerpts of Anne Sexton's poetry from The complete poems of Anne Sexton (1960, 1962, 1964, 1965, 1966, 1972, 1975, 1976) and excerpts from Diane Wood Middlebrook's biography Anne Sexton: A biography (copyright 1991, reprinted by permission of Houghton Mifflin Harcourt Publishers)
Megan Feulner and Linda Sexton at Anne Sexton's estate for permission for excerpt from interview with Anne Sexton [(1973/1985). The freak show. In S. E. Colburn (Ed.), No evil star: Selected essays]

Taylor and Francis for permission to reprint excerpts from the following:

Danielle Knafo (2012) The senses grow skilled in their craving: Thoughts on creativity and substance abuse. In Dancing with the unconscious: The art of psychoanalysis and the psychoanalysis of art.
Dustin Kahoud (2014). The double-edged pen: Omnipotent fantasies in the creativity and addictions of Stephen King. Psychodynamic Practice.

Introduction

The lure of omnipotence

> In the life of desire, we find at every turn that our most intense longings, attachments, and addictions constantly transcend their immediate objects. We ask of one another more than any person can give ... some reliable sign that there is a place for us in the world. And we pursue particular material objects and satisfactions with a zeal that they cannot and, in the end, do not sustain. Having pursued these objects, we turn away from them, in disappointment and discontent, as soon as they are within our grasp. Only the beyond ultimately concerns us. The sense of a permanent power of transcendence over all limits – of openness to the infinite – is inseparable from the experience of consciousness.
>
> Roberto Mangabeira Unger (2007)

Magic will never disappear. We need it to live because it inspires us and makes life bearable. Even in our scientific and skeptical age, we cling to magic, ritual, and fantasy. Our technological progress notwithstanding, we still fiercely devote ourselves to self-serving illusions and harbor magical beliefs. That is not to say we put stock in sorcery, the Easter Bunny, or the tricks of David Copperfield. Rather, the magic of the mind exists in the form of unconscious fantasies – in particular, omnipotent fantasies.

Unconscious mental processes – feelings, thoughts, wishes, anxieties, beliefs, fears, and mental images – arise in response to needs (Isaacs, 1948). For Freud (1914/1958b), unconscious fantasy was the "mental expression of instinctual needs." For example, his theory named unconscious fantasies of infancy as "hallucinatory wish fulfillment," a psychological response to feelings of deprivation, elicited in the absence of the caregiver or because of a lack of oral sustenance. According to Freud, in the fantasy world of infantile omnipotence the mind creates or wills the caregiver or food supply in a hallucination of need gratification (as in "If it's not there, I'll *make* it be there"). As Isaacs (1948) said, "All impulses, all feelings, all modes of defense are experienced in [unconscious] phantasies which give them mental life and show their direction and purpose" (p. 81). Omnipotent fantasies are the result of unconscious psychological responses, both normal and pathological, to the limitations of the human condition.

Smith (1986) defined omnipotent fantasies as unconscious psychological processes that instill a protective or defensive sense of "not needing to need" (p. 58), while Almond (1997) called them a "sense or fantasy of unlimited influence over aspects of the self, the object, and the external world" (p. 11). Mitchell (2002) said our commitment to maintaining a feeling of omnipotence is central to our sense of safety: "the more endangered we feel, the more control we seek" (p. 25). Becker (1973) described omnipotence as an instinctual defense against the paralyzing terror resulting from awareness of inevitable and certain death. It is a response to human helplessness, the dependence on the outside world for survival ultimately doomed by death, as we "struggle to maintain a sense of power in the face of total vulnerability" (Ellman & Reppen, 1997, p. xiii). The omnipotent fantasy "refers to a deeply nonrational cast of our minds in which we extend ourselves indefinitely in time (deathlessness) and space (obliteration or denial of the limits signified by difference or otherness)" (Shabad, 2010, p. 735).

The omnipotent fantasy answers the prime evolutionary imperatives to survive and thrive. As such, its presence pervades the human psyche as both a boon and a curse. While the imagination can enable the transcendence of limitation (as in "I can do this"), it also tempts grandiose and foolish overreach (as in "Nothing is beyond me"). The myth of Icarus beautifully epitomizes the poles of this structure: Icarus flies beyond the walls of his prison with wings fashioned by Daedalus, but in an ecstasy of transcendence perishes when he fails to heed his father's warning about flying too close to the sun. The wings and the warning represent the healthy interplay of imagination and reason, fantasy and reality, in the service of progress. The fall of Icarus depicts the result of excessive omnipotent fantasies.

Any sort of flight, whether by means of sex, drugs, or acts of creativity, can become a temptation to excess. In a secret chamber of our mind we dream of a beyond that would save us from finitude. The desire to magically transform ourselves and our surroundings is a constant element in the human psyche, showing up in myths and stories the world over, insinuating itself into the fabric of human experience, and profoundly shaping our individual lives in ways we fail to recognize. The contemporary fascination with superheroes in both children and adults testifies to the power of this desire. Year after year, the highest-grossing films feature godlike beings such as Batman, Iron Man, Wonder Woman, and the like, to feed our fantasies and satisfy our need to embody the supernatural experience of immortality.

While this need operates outside conscious awareness, its residue surfaces in everyday life, in superstitions and the cognitive "tricks" we play on ourselves. For instance, many people are not willing to plan a wedding or major event on Friday the 13th; others wish on shooting stars or knock on wood to prevent the magical materialization of a forbidden thought. Even the commonplace compulsion to say "God bless you" in response to a sneeze originates in the idea that sneezing might grant evil spirits a chance to enter the body; thus, today we continue to mindlessly ward off such a "calamity."

Some people imbue personal items with magic, such as the special article of clothing worn to ensure victory in a sports event, the gold horn to ward off the evil eye, the religious icon in the car to protect against tragedy, or the sacred ring to ensure fidelity. Private rituals are in the same category. For example, before writing, an author may engage in a consistent routine they believe gets the creative juices flowing. Rituals are part of most important human acts, and while they may simply help provide a transition from one psychic state to another – for example, a ritual before bedtime—they often are imbued with a magical power that is thought to help accomplish a task. Practically superfluous (e.g. pacing around the room for ten minutes before sitting down to write), a ritual becomes necessary when a person strongly believes in its power.

In one form or another, the belief in magic is almost universal. Even the staunchest empiricist might be heard reflecting on how their career was inspired by dreams of single-handedly conquering a disease that impacted them personally with the invention of a new medicine or technology. The great genius Albert Einstein, author of the theory of relativity, continued to pursue his dream of unified field theory, turning his back on the truth of quantum physics because it did not fit with his model. While science can turn fantasy into reality, a new discovery often begins with an overblown sense of omnipotence – a sense that may even be required to begin such work.

Some claim that the belief in God entails the abandonment of reason and flight into a fantasy of blind faith (e.g. Dawkins, 2006; Freud, 1927/1961b). In *The Future of an Illusion,* Freud (1927/1961b) argued that religion represents humanity's most universal omnipotent fantasy – a delusional defense against "the crushingly superior force of nature" (p. 21). Freud saw religion as "a system of wishful illusions together with a disavowal of reality, such as we find nowhere else but in a state of blissful hallucinatory confusion" (p. 43). In *The God Delusion,* Dawkins (2006) asserted that it is "infantile" to assume "somebody else (parents in the case of children, God in the case of adults) has a responsibility to give your life meaning" (p. 162). Although we do not necessarily embrace these views to the exclusion of all counterarguments, they highlight the implication that omnipotent fantasies may underlie the spiritual position.

The desire to stretch the limits of mere mortality colors our science and technology, art and literature, dreams and conflicts. We need look no further than social media to see the urgent need to be seen and acknowledged. People strive to demonstrate they are part of a community, connected with others, and enhance the illusion of social safety through "likes" and "re-tweets." Through the magic of Facebook, Instagram, and Twitter, we reach to *fix* the problem of a troubled and besieged existence. Unable to procure true magic, we instead toil to transform the visible and secure our inherently insecure position, hoping to calm the rumblings of existential anxieties and squelch the fears that awaken us in the middle of the night. Moreover, the desire for omnipotence – as we face threat, loss, and death – drives us to pursue meaningful goals and develop a sense of mastery. Thus, we build, heal, and fight, all the while railing against impermanence and uncertainty. The telos of our technology is to end threat, loss, and death. We owe our progress to the struggle against human limitations (Knafo & Lo Bosco, 2017).

Psychoanalytic views of omnipotence

The existence of omnipotent fantasies was first proposed in the field of psychiatry at the end of World War I. Sigmund Freud (1909/1955b) introduced the concept in a case study of a patient who became known as the Rat Man, suffering from obsessional thoughts and believing the "omnipotence of [his] wishes" would bring "evils" on his father (p. 226). In the Schreber case, Freud (1910/1957) interpreted the patient's wish for possession of both male and female genitalia as deriving from unconscious fantasies of illimitability. In *Totem and Taboo* (1913/1961c), Freud wrote about the "omnipotence of thought" in primitive cultures as steeped in the belief that the outside world could be controlled through magical knowledge (Ellman & Reppen, 1997). He compared the magical thinking of "primitive" (non-Western) peoples to the "megalomania" of psychosis, the blind infatuation of lovers, and the extreme devotion of parents toward their children. He identified overvaluation as the common thread binding these states together, an attitude marked by an inflated sense of importance, either of oneself or the love object, and an exaggerated belief in one's powers (Freud, 1914/1958b). Freud saw these illusory overvaluations as residues of our earliest, most infantile fantasies – those of limitless power and absolute perfection.

In an effort to validate Freud's ideas through her work with children, Klein (1955) developed a theoretical position that added significant breadth to his notion of omnipotent fantasies. Whereas classical and ego psychology traditions portrayed the mind as stable, coherent, and layered, Klein regarded the mind as unstable, fluid, and modifiable. According to Klein, early experience is dominated by terrifying persecutory anxieties against which omnipotent fantasies are a protective force. She described idealization and grandiosity as "manic defenses" mobilized to assuage the inherently frightening condition of abject dependence and helplessness (Klein, 1955). These defenses protect the "good" images of self and other from the destructive effects of the "bad" experiences of self and other. Klein also believed that these omnipotent fantasies provide a sense of control over the object of the child's dependence and allowed them to triumph over it through fantasy.

Drawing considerably from Klein's work, Kernberg (1975) further developed the notion of omnipotent control through his idea of the grandiose self. Kernberg describes omnipotent fantasies as defenses against early experiences of aggression in which the child experiences self and other as inherently sadistic and devalued. Those who experience chronic deprivation, invalidation, and abuse are unable to tolerate hopeful feelings and become predisposed to expecting and wanting nothing and devaluing the offering of others. Their stance is that "I am/have everything. You are/offer nothing" (p. 234). The result is the establishment of the "grandiose self" – a fiercely independent person with an inflated ego, the primary function of which is to disguise feelings of profound rejection, unworthiness, and impoverishment. The grandiose self becomes a seemingly omnipotent solution to existence in a world "devoid of food and love" (Kernberg, 1986, p. 257). The grandiose self gives rise to a "vicious circle of self-admiration, depreciation of others, and elimination of all actual dependency" (Kernberg, 1975, p. 235).

Omnipotence theory became increasingly complex in the mid-twentieth century. As divergent schools of psychoanalytic and psychological theory emerged in the United States, theoretical perspectives came into conflict about whether illusions of omnipotence reflect a pathological defense or healthy psychic life (Mitchell, 1988). For example, Winnicott (1949) considered the perceptual oscillation between the harshness of "objective reality" and the illusory splendor of "subjective omnipotence" as the signpost of mental health. In a similar vein, Kohut (1971, 1977/2009b) emphasized the child's need for caregiver mirroring in developing a sense of omnipotence supporting "healthy narcissism," assertiveness, and ambition. He argued that omnipotence is not completely relinquished in the process of growing up and considered the feeling of omnipotence provided by selfobjects as a healthy part of psychic life and a continuing need throughout the lifespan. Additionally, Kohut proposed that a lack of perceived omnipotence fostered depression, fragmentation, and self-devaluation.

The magic in creativity

The Western world has traditionally viewed creativity as magical, and artists, musicians, writers, and actors are often perceived by fans as possessing omnipotent qualities. Influential art is described as mesmerizing, groundbreaking, enchanting, and awe-inspiring. The personal meaning we derive from creating and enjoying art brings delight to our existence and gives us courage to withstand the grimmer side of reality. Imagine trying to cope with life without art, music, literature, drama, or comedy. For many theorists, omnipotent fantasies and magical thinking are central to the creative process (Becker, 1973/1997; Freud, 1909/1955b; Kohut, 1977/2009b; Rank, 1932/1989; Winnicott, 1971). Creative activities are often sublimations of omnipotent fantasies about ourselves, significant others, and the world around us. We mobilize such fantasies in a continuing effort to express and work through our subjective experiences, and creativity is an important vehicle through which these fantasies achieve materialization.

Freud (1913/1961c) also proposed that creativity finds its source in the unconscious wishes and impulses of infantile fantasies. The infant is ignorant of reality and lacks reason, so its unbridled discharge of impulses results in meaningless exercises in self-gratification. For the inspiration of primary process to manifest as creative acts, the mind must process unconscious material through the consciousness and rationality of secondary process. Therefore, according to Freud, application of the reality principle to the unconscious psyche is what separates the tantrums of a child from the emotionally evocative verses of the poet. Regarding this intermixture of primary and secondary processes in creative expression, Freud wrote that art "constitutes a region half-way between a reality which frustrates wishes and the wish-fulfilling world of the imagination – a region in which primitive man's strivings for omnipotence are still in full force" (1913/1961c, p. 188).

Rank (1929/1978) agreed with Freud about the role of unconscious fantasy in the arts, taking the premise even further in stressing the adaptive value of *illusion*. Furthermore, rather than emphasize society's role in stifling the wishes that later become fulfilled through the work of creative artists, Rank underscored the acute sensitivity of the artist to the existential reality of their situation: "With the truth, one cannot live. To be able to live one needs illusions, not only the outer illusions such as art ... but inner illusions which first condition the outer" (Rank, 1929/1978, pp. 251–252). The "outer" includes a secure sense of one's own active powers and of being able to count on the powers of others.

During the same year Rank published his existentialist theories on artistic expression, Klein (1929/2002) considered the source of creativity through her examination of infantile impulses. She regarded the source of artistic impulses as a manifestation of depressive anxiety and the wish to repair the damage inflicted on both external and internal objects. Klein saw acts of "reparation" as creative solutions that allow the infant to restore lost and damaged objects. Later Klein (1940/1988, p. 360) described how the mourning process is linked with creativity:

> We know that painful experiences of all kinds sometimes stimulate sublimations, or even bring out quite new gifts in some people, who may take to painting, writing or other productive activities under the stress of frustrations and hardships ... Such enrichment is in my view gained through processes similar to those steps in mourning.

Klein (1940/1988) proposed that, despite the child's efforts to repair their inner world, omnipotent fantasies retain powerful inborn aggressive drives. The omnipotence continues to influence sublimations and repeatedly threatens the child's attempts at reparation with destructive impulses. Instead, the child "resorts to manic omnipotence" (p. 130). Thus, although Klein saw omnipotent fantasies as constricting the creative process overall, she regarded the creative act of reparation as a powerful solution to the pain associated with loss in the depressive position.

Becker (1973/1997) combined Klein's (1940/1988) notion of "triumph" with Rank's (1929/1978) ideas about illusion and creativity. Whereas Klein suggested that creative acts of reparation allow a person to "triumph" over persecutory depressive anxiety, Becker (1973/1997) opined that humankind uses creativity to triumph over the terror and dread induced by the uncertainty and absurdity of existence. The artist "reveals the darkness and the dread of the human condition and fabricates a new symbolic transcendence over it. This has been the function of the creative deviant from the shamans through Shakespeare" (p. 220).

Two theorists particularly emphasize the value of omnipotent fantasies for creativity. Kohut (1971/2011) and Winnicott (1971) replace the traditional psychoanalytic portrayal of the narcissist as child, madman, or savage with that of the creative artist. Winnicott (1971) regarded creativity as a reimmersion in a state of "subjective omnipotence" in which illusions are pursued to the fullest extent and external reality is completely disregarded. He did not consider omnipotent fantasies as either constricting or defensive. Rather, such illusions are key to the revitalization and establishment of mental health. In his discussion of the relationship between illusion and reality, Winnicott (1971) said "creativity is the retention throughout life of something that belongs properly to infant experience: The ability to create the world" (pp. 39–40). Likewise, omnipotent fantasies in Kohut's (1971/2011) theory provide inroads into the psyche to reverse processes that have led to developmental arrest. Kohut suggested that fostering grandeur and idealization facilitates a reanimation of normal developmental processes and redirects energy into creativity: "Creative artists, and scientists, may be attached to their work with the intensity of an addiction, and they try to control and shape it with forces and for purposes that belong to a narcissistically experienced world. They are attempting to re-create a perfection that formerly was directly an attribute of their own" (Kohut, 1971/2011, Kindle locations 6260–6263).

Consider the omnipotent fantasies that inspire the work that goes into writing a book – perhaps the one you are reading at this moment. Although we (the authors) generally present as rational adults with sound judgment, the omnipotent fantasies that drive us to write may not be all that different from those we entertained as young children. At times, we may be inspired by the anticipation of presenting the book to an audience and be driven by fantasies of *impacting* others through the power of words. We imagine our *creation* being met with praise. With fantasies of transforming the world around us, we retain the motivation to create – to take on, develop, and complete somewhat intimidating undertakings. So what becomes of creative inspiration if one rigidly clings to the harsher and more realistic probabilities that much too soon one's work will be sitting on a shelf collecting dust or sold used at a bargain discount? Through a fantasy that others will be changed by words in a book – that those words will become an extension of the self through which one can live on – the flame of the creative process remains ablaze.

The magic in addiction

As a result of the ways in which creative people use omnipotent fantasies, countless lives are touched in extraordinary ways. Art in its many forms has the power to enrich our perspective, assuage our loneliness, and reawaken dormant parts of our personalities. Artists are alchemists in that they transform bitter, seemingly indigestible emotions and serve them up to audiences with bold, new, intoxicating flavors. Artists are said to have particular sensitivity to the burden of mortality (Knafo, 2012), and people are powerfully drawn to such talent that can enrapture us with tragic truths wrapped up in words and images, performances, paintings, music, and the like.

The ability to create, however, sometimes requires a high price, and many artists have used addictive substances to call their muse. In just the past decade, Heath Ledger, Michael Jackson, Whitney Houston, Amy Winehouse, Phillip Seymour Hoffman, and many other influential artists lost their lives to drugs. Artists sometimes take drugs to induce magical thinking – or thinking "outside the box." Even Freud in 1884 wrote a "Song of Praise" to his new-found experiences with cocaine (Jones, 1953, p. 84). In a letter to Martha Bernays, Freud celebrated cocaine as the "magical drug" that brought him out of a severe depression and "lifted [him] to the heights in a wonderful fashion" (p. 84). Judging from the following description of his initial experimentation with cocaine, Freud might have agreed that the psychological effects of the drug provided him with a sense of *omnipotence* – alleviating the helplessness he was experiencing in the midst of a severe depression and dramatically giving him a sense of control:

> Exhilaration and lasting euphoria, which in no way differs from the normal euphoria of the healthy person ... You perceive an increase of *self-control* and possess more *vitality* and capacity for work. ... In other words, you are simply normal, and it is soon hard to believe that you are under the influence of any drug ... Long intensive mental or physical work is performed without any fatigue.
>
> (Jones, 1953 pp. 82–83)

Although Freud never explicitly addressed omnipotent fantasies in the context of drug use, contemporary psychodynamic approaches to drug addiction acknowledge their role in theory and practice (Director, 2005; Dodes, 1990; Tatarsky, 2002; Ulman & Paul, 2006; Wurmser, 1978/1995). In a model faithful to classical psychoanalysis, Wurmser (1978/1995) placed primary emphasis on an individual's desperate need to obtain relief from a harsh and relentless superego through the use of drugs. Wurmser saw drug use as a unique type of externalization offering the individual magical, problem-solving properties and the illusion of narcissistic control. He described the defense of externalization as "the action of taking magical, omnipotent control over the uncontrollable" (p. 146). In all drug users, Wurmser stated, externalization has overriding importance as "seeking the solution to an inner problem on the outside, by action and in concrete form" (p. 146). In other words, "The addict ... believes that he can will a change within himself by ingesting some material substance" (Kazin, 1976, p. 45).

Following Wurmser (1978/1995), Dodes (1990, 2003, 2011) viewed drug abuse as an effort to reverse intolerable feelings of helplessness; the sense of power granted by the drug counterbalances the sense of helplessness felt by the individual. Dodes (1990) identified the user's need "to re-establish a sense of power" (p. 398). According to Dodes, addictive behaviors and thought processes restore a sense of omnipotence by granting individuals the power to manipulate their affective states. He described how addictive acts serve as substitutions for direct action against feelings of powerlessness.

Director (2002, 2005) highlighted the value of addressing omnipotent fantasies in drug abusers, proposing a basic but powerful idea: whether drug use attempts psychological repair, a quest for contact, or merger with significant others or is a behavior embedded in patterns of social interaction, it exists within the frame of a universal fantasy that the drug is an omnipotent or magical solution for human suffering (Director, 2005). While shaped by many determinants, chronic drug use attempts to create change in a particular, prescribed way. For Director, this implies the underlying desire to feel omnipotent. She argued that the drug "is a means to implement it [this feeling], whether with regard to effects desired in the self or others in the outside world" (Director, 2005, p. 567). She also underscored how chronic drug-seeking behavior may be an attempt to reclaim a long-lost sense of omnipotence from infancy.

Ulman and Paul (2006) contended that there is a vital link between fantasy and addiction. They described the addict as the so-called Narcissus of Greek mythology, traveling through an Alice-like wonderland depicted by Lewis Carroll: the addict "is in love with an image of the self as dissociatively altered in the reflecting pool of narcissistic fantasy and mood" (p. 4). Ulman and Paul emphasized how narcissism and addiction are unconsciously driven by an insatiable desire to recover infantile states of omnipotence. They explained how fantasy is the most primary, albeit unconscious, determinant of addiction, while what is going on in the external world plays only a secondary role (Ulman & Paul, 2006, p. 6). An archaic form of narcissism, more specifically the fantasy of existing as "a megalomaniacal self" gifted with a form of magical control, is at the unconscious root of addictions (p. xvi). Such narcissistic fantasies center on the illusion that the individual possesses magical control over psychoactive chemicals, which allows them to artificially alter their subjective reality. Thus, the addict is transformed into a sorcerer capable of manipulating the forces of human nature and beyond (p. 5).

Tatarsky (2002) proposed that for the user the addictive object – much like the exciting object – possesses "the symbolic power to cure everything," and the drug becomes the focus of the individual's desire in an attempt to address needs and feelings never fully acknowledged (p. 137). Thus, the focus of the addiction is on getting and having the addictive object rather than on finding real solutions or satisfactions for the needs driving the addictive search. Investment in the addictive object signals denial of actual needs or something very wrong not being addressed. Denial protects the individual from the anxiety or threat conjured by the deeper need. The problem is that because the drug or fantasy is not a real solution, the need is never met and the user is never satisfied. The needs get more intense, and, frequently, the addictive search intensifies (p. 137).

Although most commonly associated with psychodynamic perspectives, omnipotent fantasies in substance abuse are addressed outside the boundaries of psychoanalytic theories. Consider the attack on a sense of omnipotence in the teachings of 12-step programs of recovery such as Alcoholics Anonymous (Alcoholics Anonymous World Services, 1976; Dodes, 1990). The first of the 12 steps to recovery explicitly states: "We admitted we were powerless over alcohol – that our lives had become unmanageable" (Alcoholics Anonymous World Services, 1976). The "Serenity Prayer," traditionally adopted by 12-step programs, also incorporates a radical acceptance of human powerlessness through the recitation: "God grant me the serenity to accept the things I cannot change; the courage to change the things I can; and wisdom to know the difference" (Reinhold Niebuhr as cited in Callender, 2013). Such an assault on omnipotence is the very opposite of what the drug was intended to provide. No wonder recovery is actively avoided and highly challenging.

Even within behavioral perspectives, theories of operant conditioning account for the presence of omnipotent fantasies in the psyche of substance abusers. Consider the feelings of power and control resulting from the use of addictive psychoactive substances. The drug stops the pain (negative reinforcement) while granting euphoria (positive reinforcement). Skinner (1976) himself commented on the relevance of feelings of omnipotence in reward systems: "Frequent reinforcement builds faith. A person feels sure, or certain, that he will be successful. He enjoys a sense of mastery, power, or potency" (p. 64). A number of theorists followed Skinner in identifying the intensely gratifying psychological rewards associated with reinforcers, including feelings of control, omnipotence, and perceived self-determination (Flora, 2004; Lyng, 1990; Wood et al., 1997). Furthermore, Seligman's (1998) learned helplessness theory stresses that improvement in depression is contingent on the patient's gaining a sense of control, mastery, and self-efficacy – in other words, gaining a healthy sense of omnipotence.

In addition to behavioral studies, evidence from neurobiological research supports the claim that certain states of intoxication result in feelings of omnipotence. For instance, Koob (2011) reported that elevated dopamine levels in the brain associated with a number of drugs can induce feelings of omnipotence, providing "a sense of power, a sense of being able to do things, an immediate feeling of pleasure associated with moving and getting going and being unusually capable" (p. 1); Hart (2011) also stressed the influence of neurotransmitters in omnipotent states, noting that in manic-depressive states the nervous system oscillates between "being locked in joy-filled omnipotence and in narcissistic deflation, both mechanisms that are regulated subcortically" (p. 251). Somewhat related is Schore's (1994) suggestion that when affect-regulating structures in the orbitofrontal cortex fail to reach full maturity, the disillusionment of infantile grandiosity and omnipotence never takes place. Through the combined efforts of researchers in both neuroscience and psychoanalysis, a new movement known as *neuropsychoanalysis* was spawned (Solms & Turnbull, 2010). Combining theory and research, scientists and psychoanalysts are at a crossroads in understanding the interconnections among the physiological and psychological processes of addiction, creativity, and primitive unconscious fantasies.

Fantasies of the masses

Reports of drug addiction saturated mainstream culture at the beginning of the twenty-first century. The drug-fueled escapades of addicted celebrities such as Lindsay Lohan and Charlie Sheen often took precedence over reports on foreign relations, social reform, and public policy. In the music industry, Eminem released back-to-back albums in 2009 and 2010 titled *Relapse* and *Recovery*, chronicling his journey to the bottom of a prescription painkiller bottle and subsequent rise to sobriety. Amy Winehouse's widely popular lyrical protest against the urgings of others to "go to rehab" still haunt her family, friends, and legions of fans who mourn her loss. Dr. Drew Pinsky has become a household name through his "Reality TV" drama, *Celebrity Rehab with Dr. Drew*. Other popular addiction-themed shows include *Addicted, Intervention, My Strange Addiction*, and *Hoarders. Addiction and Art* (Santora, Dowell, & Henningfield, 2010) is a recent compilation of artwork by painters who have portrayed their own personal experiences with addiction. In literature, the addiction memoir is a new genre, gaining popularity. Through self-revelatory personal narratives, addicted writers, actors, musicians, comedians, and other creatives have begun to connect with fans like never before. *Dry* (2003) by Augusten Burroughs, *Beautiful Boy* (2008) by David Scheff, *Drinking: A Love Story* by Caroline Knapp (1996), and *Lit* by Mary Karr (2009) are just a few of over a hundred titles of addiction narratives published at the turn of the century, many of which made *The New York Times* Best Sellers list. In the world of comedy, Russell Brand's *My Booky Wook: A Memoir of Sex, Drugs and Stand-Up* (2008) and Artie Lange and Anthony Bozza's *Too Fat to Fish* (2008), among numerous others, were bestselling chronicles of drug-addicted rises to comedic stardom.

Sex addiction has become sufficiently prominent that the authors of the *Diagnostic and Statistical Manual of Mental Disorders* (*DSM-5*) are considering including it in the addictive-disorders section of future editions. Movies such as *Shame* (2011) and *Thanks for Sharing* (2012) present poignant portrayals of sex addiction, while *Men, Women and Children* (2014) explores the addictive world of internet pornography, social media, and online gaming. Prime-time TV shows, including *Sex Rehab with Dr. Drew* and *Californication* bring the realities and fantasies of sex addiction to the public while countering the stigmas typically associated with sexual promiscuity. In the world of politics, both Anthony Weiner and Elliot Spitzer destroyed their careers and personal lives because of "sexting" and escort-service addiction. Touting the slogan "make your fantasy a reality," Ashley Madison became an internet sensation as a social network where married people can find others to engage in a "discrete affair." Family actor and comedian Bill Cosby is accused by more than 50 women of having drugged and sexually assaulted them. Reports, documentaries, and news specials on the sexual escapades of Charlie Sheen, David Letterman, Tiger Woods, and others have had America glued to their screens for weeks at a time.

With each account of another talented, creative public figure locked in the shackles of an addiction, people are confronted with the same question again and again – *Why?* Why do so many brilliant and creative people seem so prone to addiction? Why do so many influential personalities find themselves irresistibly drawn to intoxicating chemicals, suffer from insatiable sexual desire, and crave the numbing, nameless pleasures of gambling, social media, video games, or pornography? Is there some underlying force that drives such ravenous hunger for inebriation beneath artistic capacities?

What is the root of addiction?

In exploring this problem, researchers often find themselves approaching the fork in the road labeled *chicken* and *egg*. Highly creative individuals likely seek intoxication for any number of reasons. The debate over whether creativity and addiction are connected remains unresolved, even as it continues to receive media attention with each new headline lamenting the loss of another influential artist. Some argue that just as there are links between creativity and mental illness (Andreasen, 2005; Knafo, 2012), addictions commonly co-occur with capacities for high levels of creativity (Director, 2005) – often connected (at least initially) to substances being used as a muse for their creative needs (Knafo, 2012). But others (Biello, 2011) are reluctant to assert a solid connection, claiming that the relationship between addiction and the artist is nothing more than a myth perpetuated by popular culture and the media.

It is true that despite the impressive list of famous artists/addicts, there are far more artists who were never addicts. Nonetheless, it is hard to ignore the accounts of addiction in the memoirs of famously creative people, and accounts of the use of psychoactive substances appearing much earlier in literature and art cannot be discounted either (Boon, 2002). For instance, in French literature, Baudelaire's (1864/1970) exposés indicate that he used intoxicating substances for varied reasons, including inducing pleasure, numbing depressive symptoms, treating syphilis, and managing physical pain. Although Baudelaire was very forthright about his feelings regarding the inherently evil nature of drug addiction, he often celebrated the use of substances as the all-powerful solution to the problems of the human condition. (Baudelaire, 1864/1970). Similarly, in letters written to his fiancée in 1848, Edgar Allen Poe characterized drugs and alcohol as the artillery of pre-emptive strikes against searing painful emotions – in particular, against a vague, indescribable sense of despair he felt nearly constantly. In one letter, Poe explained his habitual intake of powerful stimulants:

> I have absolutely no pleasure in the stimulants in which I sometimes so madly indulge ... It has been in the desperate attempt to escape ... from a sense of insupportable loneliness and a dread of some strange impending doom.
>
> (Whitman, 1922, pp. 74–75)

While some psychological understanding of drug use first found its origins in centuries past, our scientific understanding of addictive behaviors has expanded dramatically. Over the past decade, advances in neurobiology and the widespread abuse of addictive pharmaceutical medications have placed emphasis on treating addiction as a brain disease (Dodes, 2011) as opposed to understanding it as symptomatic of a psychological problem. The new edition of the *Diagnostic and Statistical Manual of Mental Disorders* (DSM-5) includes "gambling disorder" as well as a section devoted to diagnoses currently being researched for future editions, including internet gaming disorder, caffeine use disorder, and hypersexual disorder (American Psychiatric Association, 2013).

Few people outside the medical or mental health community know much about addiction, and the devaluation of approaches that address the psychological etiology and dynamics of this condition further isolates sufferers (Dodes, 2011). The medical approach presupposes that the self can be manipulated and gives priority to biological "machinery," not the human being. The saving narrative of self-understanding and self-control is replaced with the saving narrative of a pill for every problem. Understanding is relinquished in favor of control, and the leviathan pharmaceutical industry profits in a nation saturated with predatory capitalism. Diagnoses of attention deficit/hyperactivity disorder, depression, and generalized anxiety are on the rise, alongside sales of antidepressants, minor tranquilizers, and stimulant medications. In addition to its dehumanizing consequences, the medical approach to addiction ignores cultural decline in which technology replaces intimacy, sociopolitical debate substitutes for a vision that binds people together, and endless war and global instability make secure life impossible. In the rapidly growing field of addiction treatment that naively accepts the status quo, the desire for quick fixes and easy answers appears to be paradoxically growing addictive in and of itself.

This response is not surprising, since human beings are meaning- and solution-seeking creatures – traits invaluable to our capacity to survive as a species. Omnipotent fantasies have been understood as both defensive and adaptive responses to overwhelming feelings of helplessness and vulnerability (Ellman & Reppen, 1997). Since the late nineteenth century, psychoanalysts have proposed that megalomaniacal fantasies and narcissistic illusions can ignite explosive internal resources to overcome states of psychic imprisonment. Intoxicating chemicals can grant one access to an illusory world, unlocked as a "fix" for life's problems through the omnipotence of one's fantasies. The right chemicals can provide people with a limitless sense of self-efficacy and control in the face of impending doom or temporarily erase reality and soothe depression, granting euphoria and psychic relief. Drugs can access self-states that relieve the feeling of being locked into intolerable experience, but do so at the price of maintaining a false sense of self that helps the addicted person hide from the world behind a thick blanket of a transitory high.

While the term "sex addiction" is now a fixture of contemporary mainstream culture, the ravenous, insatiable hunger for "forbidden fruit" mythically began when Eve first fed an apple to Adam. The power dynamics of sexuality have long been described in terms of (omnipotent) control. Sex strives to contain a chasm of unacceptable fears – fear of the opposite sex and its genitalia, fear of vulnerability, fear of the unknown, fear of loss, fear of death – all the gray between the black and white of life. Gratifying sexual encounters can represent a victory over the judgmental and opinionated voices of significant internalized others. In short, sex offers one a fantasy of transcendence, wholeness, and perfection. Often, there is little or no love or intimacy in sex addiction. In fact, the sex addict retreats from intimacy, engaging instead in make-believe relationships that grant a grandiose sense of self that possesses illusory powers. The "magic" in the fantasies driving compulsive sex acts is found in their duality and deception: the show of power and control conceals powerlessness and terror; the avoidance of intimacy hides a terrible longing for human closeness; and the heights of excitement veils inner deadness. While the sex addict may be temporarily liberated from the constraints and limitations that society places on sexuality, they are nonetheless imprisoned by their compulsion to transform their sex life into a theater that masks the origins of their deepest pain.

Any addiction can harness the magical, transformative powers of fantasies. Stephen King once joked that his writing talent came from an addiction gene he inherited from his mother that "got rewired somewhere along the way" (Rogak, 2008, p. 156). In talking about the compulsive nature of his creative writing, King said:

> I think it's part of that obsessive deal that makes you a writer in the first place, that makes you want to write it all down. Writing is an addiction for me. Even when the writing is not going well, if I don't do it, the fact that I'm not doing it nags at me.
>
> (cited in Rogak, 2008, p. 2)

That creativity is often driven by compulsion is mostly positive. Ernest Becker (1973/1997) in his classic masterpiece, *The Denial of Death*, suggested that artwork is an ideal solution to the inevitable problems of the human condition. In particular, he believed that through the illusions that produce creative acts, humankind "triumphs" over the agonizing absurdities of existence: "The creative person becomes, in art, literature, and religion, the mediator of natural terror and the indicator of a new way to triumph over it ... This has been the function of the creative deviant from the shamans through Shakespeare" (p. 220).

Whether through sex, drugs, or creativity, individuals often retreat into the inner cocoon of omnipotent fantasies when the harshness of the human condition becomes too much to bear. Yet individuals who become involved in addictive behaviors can lose sight of the consequences of their actions – relationships are threatened, jobs are in jeopardized, finances dwindle, prison looms large, and the ultimate price may have to be paid – of illness and death. When the drug or sexual conquest becomes the sole object of importance, all other realities are denied or minimized by comparison. In addiction, users find themselves in a place where *the illusions themselves become addictive*, and they become unable to relinquish them (Mitchell, 2000). One of the major barriers to the successful treatment of addictions is the unquestionable fact that drugs and sex can be intensely euphoric, pleasurable, and intoxicating, recreating the world and dramatically altering the sense of self. In the pages that follow, the authors examine the interactions among sex, drugs, and creativity as well as how narcissistic illusions fuel both art and addiction.

Part I of this volume examines omnipotent fantasies as a theoretical construct that can be seen as the ground of creativity and addiction. We focus on how unconscious fantasies fuel the addictive behaviors of creative individuals, and how such human responses are wielded like a double-edged sword against the pains of existence – offering the potential to both inspire creativity and fuel compulsive drug use. In an effort to better understand the nuances in this relationship, we examine the quality of the fantasies from which both creative processes and addictive behaviors emerge. We cast a light on the origins of unconscious, omnipotent fantasies that drive the search for a magical solution to the inherent problems of the human condition. In our elucidation of how unconscious fantasies tint the lenses through which we perceive ourselves and the world, we illustrate both the richness and the grandiosity of magical illusions. We review theoretical and empirical research and elaborate on how mental magic is cultivated and projected into our environment in multifaceted responses to the pleasures, dangers, and paradoxes of life.

"The sexual illusionist: sleeping with a fantasy" (Chapter 1) introduces omnipotent fantasies of breaking through the boundaries of human sexuality, thus transforming and expanding the limitations of mortality. Sex can serve multiple defensive or adaptive functions, such as the avoidance of intimacy and the retreat from uncontrollable relationships. Compulsory behavior, often found in the perversions, therefore, is not merely about sex; it is ultimately about substituting a sense of empowerment for one of humiliation and replacing a sense of inner deadness with sexual excitement. The ingeniousness of such behavior lies in its ability to transform trauma into pleasure and risk into desire. Case examples are presented to show how omnipotent fantasies play out in sexual life, often of the same kind motivating the creation of art. The work and lives of Alfred Hitchcock, Mick Jagger, Pablo Picasso, Georges Simenon, and Anaïs Nin illustrate how creativity and compulsive sexuality intersect.

"Elixirs of immortality: transformations of intoxication" (Chapter 2) explores how omnipotent fantasies find expression in the compulsive pursuit of intoxicating substances. Fantasies tantalize users, drawing them into spirals of substance abuse. Several theorists have written about the ways narcissistic illusions can incite a frantic, addictive search for a magical substance that silences the rumblings of existential anxiety. This chapter also explores the insights and reflections of famous writers – including Anne Sexton, John Cheever, Charles Bukowski, Stephen King, Caroline Knapp, and Mary Karr – who describe the fantastical manifestations of drug-addled experiences.

"Mightier than the sword: the magic of creativity" (Chapter 3) turns to the creative process and describes the ways in which omnipotent fantasies find expression in torrents of words, images, and musical intonations. Fantasies of early childhood materialize in disparate forms of art and are often largely unconscious efforts to gratify human desires for control, intimacy, validation, and acceptance, and to contain furious strivings and intolerable fits of rage. Significant to understanding creative processes, unconscious fantasies often function as the "man behind the curtain" of creative behaviors (Ghent, 1999; Klein, 1929; Novick & Novick, 2003; Phillips, 1998; Segal, 1974; Wurmser, 1978/1995). This chapter also explores the frequent connection between artistic creativity and the use of substances. It further addresses how omnipotent fantasies driving creativity – as well as creative behaviors – have the potential for becoming addictive.

Part II of this volume brings theory to life through narratives unearthed in literary and clinical case histories. Creative writers who live with addiction have generally not been shy about telling their experiences in personal narratives such as journals, memoirs, letters, interviews, and poetry. Additionally, creative writers have developed a unique reputation over time for their extraordinary sensitivity and attunement to their internal worlds and fantasy lives (Knafo, 2012). Because of the nature of the writing profession, there are countless writers who have spun their experiences into rich and insightful literary tapestries for public consumption. Due to the recent surge in popularity of addiction memoirs, there is no shortage of autobiographical accounts reflecting on the multifaceted aspects of addictive dynamics.

With the help of the reflections of celebrated writers and the clinical case featured in Part II, we breathe life into theory, illustrating how omnipotent fantasies of magically transforming oneself find paradoxical pathways to expression – both self-destructive cycles of addictive behavior and artistic endeavors. Individual chapters present the personal revelations of Anne Sexton and Stephen King, respectively – who both wrote extensively about the omnipotent fantasies that drove their creative processes as well as their addictive behaviors. Chapter 7 explores a case history in which a patient used sex, drugs, and creativity as magical solutions to alleviate the pain of lifelong trauma. The Conclusion delineates the conditions from which either creativity or addiction emerges while also illustrating how maladaptive, rigidly held illusions can coexist alongside flexible, healthy illusions that foster creativity.

Through this presentation of the theoretical constructs describing omnipotent fantasies in sexuality, addiction, and creativity, along with the illustrative narratives and clinical material, we hope to open a window on a vast landscape of meaning with regard to human motivation. Whether omnipotent fantasies result in self-destructive cycles of addictive behavior and/or artistic endeavors depends on how a person relates to those fantasies themselves. Although we may not be able to live without magic, it is important to know where it originates from and why and what heavens and hells it can conjure.

Part I

The magical imperative

Chapter 1

The sexual illusionist

Sleeping with a fantasy

> Sex is, directly or indirectly, the most powerful weapon in the armoury of the magician.
>
> Aleister Crowley (1973)

From the cradle to the grave, human sexuality is infused with magic and fantasy and possesses an omnipotent dimension. The mystery of sexuality involves the secrets that desire keeps and the illusions it fosters. Whether we know it or not, our sex lives are crowded with relationships from the past: those who loved us, abused or deprived us, humiliated us, treated us with kindness, seduced us, or were forbidden to us. Representations of these people, their functions in our lives, and the relationships we had with them enter into the intrigue of the adult sexual theater. Every temptation, every choice of stimulation, every ritual of excitement, and every climax is influenced by the past and cloaked in its shadow. Adult sexuality is the way we master, act out against, and make reparation to the figures from our past. Since these relationships psychologically constitute sexuality's hidden agendas, participants are usually completely unaware of the symbolic sorcery operating just beneath the surface of their most passionate, concrete acts.

Freud (1905/1953; 1930/1961d) placed human sexuality at the center of psychoanalytic theory, proposing that civilization subjugates human drives in the service of culture. He further explained why human sexuality is infused with fantasy. Freud believed children to be polymorphously perverse – that is, able to be excited by anyone or anything – and to express their sensuality through a variety of erogenous zones (1911/1958a). Moreover, since human beings have no direct outlet for their sexual drives until much later in their development, they learn to seek satisfaction by turning inward toward fantasy rather than outward toward reality (Freud 1911/1958a). Thus, it is not surprising that people attribute magical powers to their sexuality, making it more than an instinctual act by imbuing it with secret uniqueness. This can even become a cultural practice, as in the case of female foot binding in China, which sacrificed the woman to permanent handicap in the service of a defensive chimera. The foot, the body part closest to the ground and easily soiled, is altered through crippling mutilation and recast as fetish of exotic splendor and highly charged eroticism. Sex, the act of an animal, is transformed through the power of human imagination and banished – by concealing it in the fetish.

Sex can elevate mood (Goliszek, 2014) and boost self-esteem (Mastro and Zimmer-Gembeck, 2015) and has a major role in sustaining or dissolving relationships (Perel, 2006). The uses of sex can be constructive or destructive: address trauma, enact revenge, heal an injured psyche, avoid intimacy, cultivate love, foster addiction, and challenge mortality. For example, suicide missions are sometimes driven by fantasies of sexual rewards in the afterlife (72 virgins in heaven promised to the faithful by the Quran). More pedestrian fantasies are reproduction missions in which children fulfill an omnipotent fantasy for parents who hope to gain immortality through their progeny (Wisman & Goldenberg, 2005).

Unlike animals, human beings are both sexual *and* erotic. As a result, imagination plays a central role in human sexual congress, which carries the burden of symbolic meaning and unconscious expression. Morin (1995) wrote that our "erotic landscape is vastly larger, richer, and more intricate than the physiology of sex" (p. 2). The erotic refers to the meaning people attach to their sexuality, including their objects of attraction and what they find arousing. Indeed, it is the mind that creates, intensifies, focuses, or limits our sexual passions. Sex is a drive, but Eros – "the source of attraction and the craving for sexual love" – is highly individual and animated by the totality of human drama (p. 2).

Ernest Becker (1973), saw an inherent problem in human sexuality because the animal body and the ephemeral and highly symbolic self cannot be fully integrated. The erotic transformation of the animal act can never successfully banish the vulnerable and doomed animal, destined for death. In addition, sexual behaviors are often taboo and, therefore, intimately connected with the morals and mores of society. Most cultures historically have forbidden sexuality until adulthood, and then often only within a heterosexual marital relationship. Paglia (1990) claimed that these limits on sexuality result in the near impossibility of an anxiety-free human sexual act.

Further complicating matters is the observation that sexual mores and morals change over time and place. Homosexuality, for example, once labeled a perversion, is no longer considered so by many in the United States; it was removed from the *Diagnostic and Statistical Manual of Mental Disorders* (DSM) and gay marriage has been legalized. Once thought taboo, sadomasochism has gone mainstream with the popularity of E. L. James's *Fifty Shades of Grey*, a romantic S&M trilogy. Sex dolls and sex robots are proliferating (Knafo & Lo Bosco, 2017). And a third of young Japanese have chosen to forgo intimate relationships in favor of celibacy or technology-based relating, claiming relationships are *mendokusai*, simply too much trouble (Haworth, 2013).

All of these factors contribute to the complexity of Eros. Whereas the sexual act is simple and straightforward, Eros – enigmatic and paradoxical – raises endless questions. How do our childhoods influence the sexual beings we become? Why do many people not desire the partner they love? Why is forbidden love so alluring? Why are relationships less sexually charged when partners share equal power? How does our unconscious shape our sexuality? Sexual perversion is even more mysterious, a veritable Pandora's box of erotic secrets.

In perversion, sex can be an outlet for creativity and aggression (Bach, 1994; Knafo & Lo Bosco, 2017; Chasseguet-Smirguel, 1984; Stoller, 1975); it can also be used to defend against anxiety, fear, and trauma (Stoller, 1974, 1975). Knafo & Lo Bosco (2017) define perversion as a universal tendency among human beings, a repeated enactment of a scripted behavior whose purpose is mastering trauma. Usually (but not always) sexual, this behavior casts a grand illusion showcasing the actor's uniqueness and specialness while hiding the conquest of the trauma. Thus, the actor becomes a magician who transforms misery into pleasure (Knafo & Lo Bosco, 2017). Perversion is found in any human system whose aim, purpose, or meaning is – by the very operation of that system – reversed, undermined, violated, or destroyed (Knafo & Lo Bosco, 2017).

Every person engaging in a perversion spins a magical illusion masking an underlying psychic stalemate. The word *magic* is used intentionally; like the illusionist who creates an impression that the laws of nature have been suspended (e.g. cutting a woman in half; levitating), the sexual illusionist is compelled to conceal pain in a magic show in which psychological pain suddenly disappears. This chapter examines how sexuality and creativity are used to cast an illusion of omnipotence. Sexual perversion best illustrates the connection between Eros and omnipotent fantasies, which is why it is the focus of this discussion.

Perversion and spell casting

Perversion is related to unconscious fantasies that disavow reality and create illusions that impart fake power. Perversions may grant an illusory penis to a woman, render a child an equal sexual partner, or bring a corpse back to life. The magic is found in the duality of the deception: the show of power and control conceals powerlessness and terror; the avoidance of intimacy hides a terrible longing for human closeness; and the heights of excitement veil an inner deadness.

For many, the term "perversion," calls to mind the derogatory label of "pervert" – a pejorative designation loaded with moral judgment and righteous condemnation. The verb *pervert* is defined as "an effort to alter (something) from its original course, meaning, or state to a distortion or corruption of what was first intended" (Oxford University Press, 2009), but the noun *pervert* came to mean a person engaging in abnormal or unacceptable sexual behavior and is associated with sin and evil. Not surprisingly, psychological theory examining the phenomenon was tainted with prior religious ideas about perversion (Knafo & Lo Bosco, 2017). Although *sin* was replaced with *pathology*, perverts were still seen as sinners, monsters, devils, and abominations, and their acts were characterized as filthy, evil, and sick. The most commonplace images associated with this term include the "dirty old man" in a raincoat flashing young women on the street, or the "creep" waiting on the playground to prey on an innocent child. Thus, "normal" people stood on one side, viewing and judging *them* – the "perverts" – who stood on the other side. This clearly delineated binary is a religious inheritance that does not properly recognize the ubiquity of perverse proclivities and perverted sexual *and* social enactments.

Neither life nor human sexuality conforms to either/or, this or that, good or evil. Many people may enjoy productive, happy, intimate relationships, yet sometimes engage in consensual "kinky" sex, basking for a time on a small island of ecstasy with their lovers, as far from the madding crowd as one can get. But when perverse behaviors become the mainland, centering on a rigid script necessary to produce excitement, then they enter the realm of what Knafo and Lo Bosco (2017) call *perversion proper*. These authors propose that sexuality exists on a spectrum, with the far end associated with behavior that is increasingly imbued with objectification, compulsion, hostility, vengeance, and even danger. In this context, perversion may be fueled by omnipotent fantasies that overlap with those driving addictions to substances, obsessive-compulsive behaviors, and even psychopathy.

Perversion theory helps explain how the repression of loss, tragedy, and grief becomes pitched to an intolerable level. Psychosexual scripts that disguise trauma behind the veil of a pleasurable and highly symbolic act attempt to master that trauma through the pleasure itself. Keep in mind that such a script may even preclude physical sex, as in the case of some mothers who pervert their relationship with their child by treating their offspring as an extension of themselves (Welldon, 1988). A stereotypical example of this behavior is stage mothers who enroll their children in beauty pageants from a very young age. The son or daughter is now a mere self-object, a symbolic phallus expressing power and freedom the mother lacks. For such a female, the perverse illusion is about overcoming the trauma of incompleteness, of not being and not having, of replacing ugliness with beauty, powerlessness with power, emptiness with meaning, boredom with excitement, and mediocrity with excellence. (Knafo, 2010). Because the script fails to completely resolve the underlying issue of injury and loss, it must be continually repeated, which is similar to the way in which an addict must return to their drug.

Perhaps the deepest problem in perversion is the struggle with intimacy – experiencing the other as a living and whole self, a unique subject with their own desires, wishes, and dreams. All human beings hunger for intimate relationships and want to be deeply connected and essential to another, whether sex is involved or not. And therein lies the difficulty, for the more deeply joined we are to another person – that is, the greater the intimacy – the more the possible loss of the other becomes a threat to our existence, and thus the greater our need to shape them into a desirable object. People necessarily objectify others to some degree to satisfy their needs, which always involves a fantasy. How ironic that the need to be close, to be joined, is central to the very disconnection that erodes intimacy. The slide toward perversion occurs in the intensification of this objectification and the narrowing of its scope, such that the psycho-emotional encounter with the other must occur through an increasingly rigid script, subjecting the other to an *object only* status. For example, Bach's (1994) theory of sadomasochistic relations centers on the omnipotent defenses enlisted against the experience of object loss. He believed that sadomasochists choose to suffer and live in pain rather than experience object loss. Sadists deny dependence on objects who have failed them in the past. They identify with an idealized version of the mother who gave them pain while at the same time denying their need for her. Bach (1994) imagined the sadist's fantasy as: *I can do anything I want to you, and you won't leave me.* His script is: *If I make you feel as badly as I do, then I know you love me, and we can retrieve our lost togetherness.* The sadist experiences sexual satisfaction from recapturing the lost love object and punishing it for straying. Conversely, the masochist's script is: *You can do anything you want to me as long as you don't leave me.* In both cases, the pain of suffering is a defense against the greater pain of loss. In exchange, control results in dehumanization and a master–slave relationship. The case study that follows further illustrates how perversion is used to defend against the mental anguish of object loss.

Perversion as a cover-up: Yaffa's dilemma

Yaffa, a patient of DK (Knafo), met Lenore in Paris at a small café in view of the Eiffel Tower looming darkly under a graying sky. Each was alone at her small table, Lenore sipping Merlot and Yaffa nursing her coffee. A game of subtle flirtation began between the two women, until Lenore beckoned with her forefinger. Soon the two women were talking with great animation, leaning forward toward each other, already assuming the posture that suggested they would soon cross intimate boundaries.

Yaffa, an Israeli woman in her 30s, was on vacation from her job as a schoolteacher, but she quickly left her life behind to follow Lenore, an American woman in her 50s, to the United States to help her with her yoga center. For a short while, Yaffa felt the happiest she had ever been in her life. This gradually changed, as Lenore became critical of Yaffa, teasing her about her accent and fashion sense, correcting her grammar and posture, disapproving of the time she spent on the phone with family members, and offering increasingly harsh feedback on Yaffa's meditation classes. Yaffa reacted by trying to please her host, but this only seemed to incur even more criticism. By degrees, criticism became rebuke and rebuke became mockery.

This same pattern of change also played out in the bedroom. Lenore had been the dominant partner from the beginning, but now she began to command her partner throughout the sex act and gradually incorporated rough play – spankings and bondage – into their lovemaking. At first Yaffa was hesitant but she soon surrendered to the demands that transformed Lenore from her lover into her mistress. She excitedly submitted to the demands of her mistress, drawing her pleasure from pleasing Lenore. Under Lenore's tutelage she wore the "slave" clothing of the older woman's choosing, allowed herself be tied at the ankles and wrists to the bed frame, and became completely obedient to erotic direction.

As the days passed, Lenore shaped Yaffa into a live-in slave. She took classes away from Yaffa, who was relegated to the role of house cleaner. Lenore's mockery turned into humiliation and bondage, with shrill and demeaning criticism of Yaffa's every word and behavior. She told her she could no longer call her family, took away two of the three rooms she had initially given her for use in the large house, and provided a long list of menial chores for Yaffa to perform daily. Yaffa's mind became totally centered on her mistress's desires; she thought of nothing else and believed that Lenore would soon warm to her and again return some of the great love she felt for her partner. Yet each evening when Lenore returned home, she criticized Yaffa's work and even punished her if she was deeply displeased. The punishments varied, depending on Lenore's moods; Yaffa might be spanked, or sent to her room, or made to kneel in the middle of the floor and ask for forgiveness, or be stripped of her clothing for the rest of the evening. Sex would sometimes take place at this time. Whereas once Lenore returned the pleasure given to her by Yaffa, she was now told to pleasure herself. Eventually, she was disallowed even this pleasure, and her desire for Lenore was mocked. Lenore might brush against her or display her breasts or derrière, or talk suggestively to indicate she wanted sex. "Beg me for it," she'd say, and Yaffa would comply, only to be laughed at and ridiculed for her desire. Sometimes when she reacted to the ridicule with tears, Lenore became excited.

"What are you, Yaffa?" Lenore asked.

"I am your lover," she responded.

Lenore grabbed her hard by the hair and pulled her close. "No, you are something else. Tell me what it is."

"I am your slave."

"Yes. Now you may pleasure me."

Yaffa felt stripped of her dignity, but her attachment to her mistress was unbreakable. The thought of Lenore abandoning her took her breath away, and many a night she lay awake wondering how she might encourage an exchange of real love. In one part of herself, she knew that her lover would never treat her with anything but cruelty and indifference. She'd become a willing slave, yet she felt depressed and ashamed. Even if she could call her family, what could she tell them? She had no job, no money, no friends, and she had become completely dependent on Lenore. In another part of herself, she believed that Lenore truly loved her and reasoned that if she didn't, she wouldn't continue the relationship.

Many of us have trouble understanding how an intelligent and talented woman like Yaffa would agree to submit to so much abuse. Why do battered women stay in relationships with abusive husbands? Common sense tells us that punitive behavior will lessen the likelihood of a behavior being repeated. It would seem that when we are punished, we wish to avoid or escape the behaviors that would result in additional punishment. But punishment can at times create a paradoxical effect by maintaining or even increasing the unde-sired behavioral response. This is usually the case when punishment is paired with affection (Reid et al., 2013). As a result, the punished person learns to associate pain with love. By degrees Lenore had convinced Yaffa to become a slave, to draw pleasure from degradation and humiliation, a dark magic – indeed a kind of spell from which Yaffa could not free herself. Yaffa carried responsibility for her plight in that she colluded in this perverse pact (Stein, 2005). Here, two magicians staged a show, not one.

Fantasies of omnipotence were central to the relationship between these two necromancers. In the beginning, they created a show that seemed to them unique and transcendent, an erotic wonderland of exquisite pleasure see-mingly founded on love. Their relationship felt extraordinary, beyond the grasp of mere mortals. Yet, even when that illusion became tattered, omni-potent strivings did not cease. Yaffa still granted her mistress *total control* and continued to believe in her own power to regain a love that did not exist in the first place. For her part, Lenore, the god in the relationship, exercised her power with increasing cruelty. Their drama, like many staged in the sadoma-sochistic theater, resembled one between an angry, jealous god and a miser-able supplicant hungering for redemption. Since even in conventional relationships that eschew such narrow extremity, sadomasochistic elements play a role in ramping up interest and excitement between partners; the affair between Lenore and Yaffa has much to teach about the motivating force of omnipotent fantasy.

In Yaffa's case, it became clear that childhood factors played a major role in her choice of partner. Her attraction to older women indicated her desire for a mother figure. Yaffa's father died when she was a child, and she became very attached to her mother. They did everything together, even sleeping in the same bed. Although Yaffa described her mother as a cold and unfeeling woman, she worried when Yaffa went out, so Yaffa agreed to stay home, which resulted in her mother becoming the center of her life. Control and emotional abuse became the norm for her. To fall asleep, she imagined hitting herself on the head with a hammer. This fantasy calmed her and even felt pleasurable.

When Yaffa was ten, her mother had a child with a man and "replaced" her with this infant sister who now became mother's new favorite. Yaffa never overcame the pain and rage of being supplanted by her sibling. Her relationships with older women became a way of trying to recapture her lost union with her mother and mastering her childhood traumas: her father's death, which she experienced as abandonment, and her mother's shifting affections, which she also experienced as loss. From early in her life, Yaffa felt caught between the pain of two bad choices: giving up her mother or living with a less-than-good mother. She chose the latter, although her consciousness was divided. She knew she was mistreated and suffered terribly. Yet she simultaneously held on to a fantasy of union with her idealized partner who would never leave her as her mother and father had. If she surrendered to Lenore, she maintained the fantasy that her mother/partner was dependable and infallible. After Lenore kicked Yaffa out of her home, Yaffa finally returned to her mother's home in Israel. She knew she needed help and so she began therapy. She told DK over and over again that when Lenore held her, she felt at home. Typical of masochists, Yaffa took all the blame for the way her relationships turned out: "I suck the passion out of relationships; everything I get close to dies."

Treatment helped Yaffa see the parallels between her relationship with her mother and her relationship with Lenore. When she was not with her, she felt dead. When she was mistreated, she felt alive and learned that "this is love." Little by little, Yaffa came to realize that what she was calling love was her way of avoiding mourning over her childhood losses. "I am inaccessible to intimacy," she observed astutely. "My problem is a fundamental intimacy problem."

Yaffa gradually recognized how abandoned she had felt for years. "I always felt alone without a safety net," she said. She also realized how she used her relationships with older sadistic women to avoid facing her losses and holding on to whatever life she had left in her. She magically transformed the pain of loss and abuse into an excitement that fueled her pleasure but, more important, one that made her feel connected to life. Eventually, Yaffa used the therapy to express her sadness and anger toward her parents and to mourn the losses she had experienced in childhood. As she accomplished this, love became disassociated with pain, and Yaffa was finally able to let go of the type of relationship she had with her mother and Lenore.

Perversion and omnipotence

Perversion is the ideal psychological structure and behavioral enactment from which to comprehend the omnipotent power of illusion that exists in human sexuality. Personal trauma, childhood history, and sexual and social development are important for understanding perversion. Stoller (1974, 1975) agreed with Freud that perversion originates in childhood, but added to Freud's theory by explaining how children who undergo humiliation, debasement, and trauma are more likely to develop perversions because they need to reverse and repair the events of their childhood. The script of the perverse fantasy and behavior, said Stoller, includes a hidden agenda of revenge and repair aimed at converting childhood trauma into adult mastery.

Green, Stoller, and MacAndrew (1966), who interviewed a number of transvestites, presented a typical example of a male transvestite who was humiliated as a child for not being masculine enough and forced to wear female clothing. His core male identity was threatened at an early age when he was defenseless. As an adult, this same man now found pleasure in dressing up like a woman. His cross-dressing was no longer experienced as traumatic but, rather, had become his major source of pleasure. It was as if he was saying to his prior abusers: "You can dress me as a girl, but I am still a man. I am still intact, no matter how many girls' clothes you put on me. I still have my penis!" According to Stoller (1975), such perversions involve risk because they go back to the site of the trauma. But in this instance, the cross-dresser felt triumphant because he had transformed this old danger into excitement. Stoller called the effects of such behavior "magic bullets" created to supply the illusion of an instant cure that conceals a deep hurt. What Stoller doesn't note is the implication that this magic is created by a godlike being who can alter reality with a wish and a gesture.

The magic in perversion is found in transforming pain to pleasure. Behind the scenes at the theater of perversion are duality and deception, in which pleasure and desire are married to trauma and revenge. On one hand, the perverse believe themselves freer (or happier, or better-off) than others, because they are not constrained by the limitations that govern behavior; their lives are imbued with erotic radiance, and they become god among mortals. On the other hand, they are imprisoned by their compulsions to transform their sexual life into a tightly scripted and staged production that masks the origins of deep pain.

Sexual mastery of death

Sexual perversion has an additional dimension, which is its role in the human animal's overcoming death. Not surprisingly, and the degree of childhood trauma notwithstanding, everyone shares in splitting, castration anxiety (in the broadest sense of loss of autonomy, self-control, and the power of agency), disavowal, rage, and rituals and scripts that create the illusion of mastery and control. Everyone is to some degree perverted because perversion is a universal response to the trauma of human helplessness and limitation (Knafo & Lo Bosco, 2017).

Many theorists note a close relationship between perversion and attempts to deny or control death and deadness. A major proponent of this view was Ernest Becker (1973), who viewed perversion partly as a protest against species sameness and fear of the body with its accompanying threat of disease and mortality. In his words, "the fetish takes 'species meat' and weaves a magic spell around it" (p. 236). For the fetishist, the body is no longer flesh; it becomes ethereal, freed from decay and death. The carnal body thus becomes the symbolic body, the body capable of transcending mortality. Becker considered "man-made fetishes" – things and symbols rather than the body – to be tools for prevailing over the natural order, taming it, and making it safe. He regarded perversions as ingenious in their transformation of pain and death into ecstasy and vitality. His theory locates perversion as a core presence within the human sexual and social condition.

Chasseguet-Smirguel (1983) similarly opined that perversion is an effort to escape the fragile human condition, a need to become the Master, thus denying helplessness, dependency, castration, and death. Ogden (1995) and McDougall (1972) viewed perversion as an illusionary attempt to experience excitement and vitality while filling a deadening void left by the real or fantasized loveless union of the parents. It is, Ogden (1995) said, a futile attempt to extract life from death, truth from falsehood.

Some theorists focus on the enlivening purpose of perversion. For example, Kramer-Richards (2003) said that perversion results in aggression at the service of correcting the cruel mother or restoring the dead one. Welldon (2009, 2011) defined perversion as a manic defense against the black hole of depression and suicide, calling it the "erotization of death" (2011, p. 35). She even described perversion as "dancing with death" (2009), a concealed desire to avoid the painful awareness of an unresolved mourning process. Georges Bataille (1957) viewed perverse sexuality as both an attempt to overcome death and, with the sex act's dissolution of boundaries, a way of simulating and transcending it. He believed that the excess of erotic life results in ecstatic union of self and world, the merging of organic and inorganic matter, and the experience of overcoming one's solitude and existential dread. Therefore, intense transgressive sexual acts simultaneously mimic and defy death, rising above it in the act of climax. Indeed, autoerotic asphyxiation is an obvious case in point.

The common thread that unites these views is the existential and universal problem of being a conscious animal, a being aware of its inevitable death and repressing and/or fleeing the pervasive terror of this awareness. Sex is linked to life *and* death, the former through procreation, the later through miserable inevitability. Thus, sex is easily and unconsciously employed in the battle against mortality, hijacked by fantasies of omnipotence to transform the symbolic elements of the act into cries of protest and quests for transcendence. In the words of one of DK's patients, "Let's be honest. Hot sex is a fistfight with death. Cold sex is death itself. Most people prefer the former even if they don't have the guts. You go down in either case. But with hot sex at least you go down in flames of glory." The same patient once stated that without some degree of perversion, sex becomes a bore.

Illusions of resurrection: the case of Count von Cosel

Extreme necrophilia surely casts a harsh light on the dark side of the link between sex and death and illustrates the perverse use of omnipotent illusions to defend against loss and mortality (Knafo, 2015). The story of Count von Cosel, born Karl Tanzler in Dresden, Germany, is a case in point. He arrived in Florida in 1927, and while employed as an X-ray technician and bacteriologist at Marine Hospital in Key West, he met Elena Milagro Hoyos, a beautiful 20-year-old of Cuban descent who was dying of tuberculosis (Harrison, 2009). Since the age of 12, von Cosel had experienced apparitions and dreams of a woman he later believed was Elena, and he became convinced that she was meant to become his bride. After they met, von Cosel became obsessed with her, lavishing her with gifts. He also devised his own methods to cure her, which included electric shock treatment and special potions. Hearing a romantic song, "La Boda Negra" (The Black Wedding), about a man who dug up the body of his lover who died before they wed, may have planted a seed in von Cosel's mind. On one occasion, he wrote to Elena, "If you were a mummy, five thousand years old, I would marry you just the same" (Harrison, 2009, p. 50). He appointed himself as Elena's guardian angel and he transported his pipe organ to her family's home to sing and play the songs he wrote to express his undying love; he also played Wagner's opera *Parsifal*, describing love in its most divine form as taking place after death (Harrison, 2009).

Elena died at 22, and von Cosel planned and paid for the funeral. He perceived the funeral procession as a wedding march and, rather than experiencing the death as an ending, he saw it as a new beginning: "Now at least nobody could take my Elena away from me," he wrote in his diary (Harrison, 2009, p. 67). He could not tolerate the thought of her body deteriorating underground, so he designed and built an ornate mausoleum for her, inscribed with his name as well as hers. Every night, he sat by her coffin, talking to her and believing she was asking him to release her from her prison so they could be reunited. Two years later, von Cosel finally removed her body from the crypt and placed her in the cabin of an old airplane he was working on situated behind the hospital in which he was employed. Eventually, he bought a shack on deserted Rest Beach, Florida, so he could place her on his bed and dress her in a wedding gown and serenade her with his homemade organ. He slept with her for the next seven years (Harrison, 2009).

Naturally, Elena's body rapidly decomposed once exposed to the elements, challenging von Cosel to draw on his scientific and creative skills to restore and maintain the corpse. He replaced the corpse's rotted eyes with glass eyes, made a wig from its falling hair, used piano wire to string the bones together, stuffed the cadaver with rags to keep it from collapsing, treated the skin with a mixture of wax and silk, and drenched the corpse in perfumes. Entertaining omnipotent delusions, von Cosel was certain that his efforts would eventually bring his love back to life. In the meantime, he inserted into what was left of the corpse's vagina a tube wide enough to permit sexual intercourse (Harrison, 2009).

It is difficult but essential to imagine the level of obsession involved in this perversion, the effort and action required to sustain the fantasy of dialogue and relationship with a decomposing corpse, the doomed effort to resurrect a life where none can exist. But only through such extreme acts of imagination and an understanding of the omnipotent defense is it possible to get past the initial reaction of disgust that jettisons deeper considerations from the mind. Only then is it possible to appreciate the underlying existential desperation of such failed psychological strategies. The Count was fighting death while he was having sex with death, taking the denial of death, something we all do, to its most radical extreme: "For me she will never die but will live on with me, and I shall always treat and respect her as a living person" (Harrison, 2009, p. 105), he wrote. These superhuman efforts to bring Elena back to life were, very likely, attempts to re-find and join the lost mother of von Cosel's childhood. His true madness is in what his ghoulish acts conceal: a bankrupt program of human transcendence. He continued his perverse honeymoon for seven years and would have done so indefinitely had not Elena's sister Nana followed rumors to von Cosel's home and discovered with horror the cadaver of her sister. Von Cosel was arrested but soon set free due to the expiration of the statute of limitations on his crime. He himself was found dead in 1952, slumped next to a wax replica that wore Elena's death mask (Harrison, 2009).

Those with perversions like von Cosel's, might, at first glance, seem not to fear death but rather to enjoy it. In fact, the fear of death is converted into a sexual attraction to death, which then provides a false sense of mastery over it. As with other perversions, von Cosel felt his actions imbued him with a sense of uniqueness and specialness. He was not like ordinary humans; laws or taboos did not apply to him. He did not flee the Grim Reaper but ran toward him (in the form of a female). He took the unbearable, horrific, complicated, contaminated, anarchic, difficult, ugly, and abject and transformed it into something simple, pure, ordered, easy, beautiful, and harmonious (Kristeva, 1982). It would be difficult to find a better illustration of the omnipotent defense than this one. Perversion touches on what is most human in us, revealing the existential struggle in which we all engage, and no human being is entirely free from its shadow. Personal trauma is almost certain, but existential trauma is guaranteed to all. Death is the final castration, the skeleton's victory.

Indeed, Count von Cosel's attempt to bear a loss and resurrect a love is something we all do, albeit in less extreme ways. Reality is harsh, and the reality of loss and death is the harshest experience we must bear. Illusions are embedded in love relationships; fantasies are integral parts of sexual relationships; and omnipotence in the service of warding off death and continuing preserving a bond of love are all too human.

Magic wands

The word *fetish* derives from the Portuguese term *feitiço* and was originally associated with artificiality (Iacono, 2016). Charles de Brosses coined the term "fetishism" in 1757 to describe the earliest stage of religious belief: the attribution of magical powers to an object (de Brosses, Morris & Leonard, 2017). Almost all religions, from Voodoo to Catholicism, attribute special powers to objects. Fetishes obviously draw on omnipotent fantasies, especially sexual fetishes, which sexualize an object by psychologically imbuing it with the power of sexual attraction, sometimes to such a high degree that the object substitutes for a sexual encounter with another person. Anything in the world can be eroticized – shoes, stockings, fur, hats, smoking women who play with balloons – and, yes, even trees and bicycles! In some sense, we all have fetishes – objects we are attached to or even addicted to, objects we worship and attribute special powers to, objects we need to make us feel soothed or pleasured. In our daily lives, most of us would feel lost or incomplete without our laptops, cell phones, tablets, and iPads, many of which are also used for sexual purposes (e.g. sexting or porn addiction). The current proliferation of technology facilitates fetishistic relating, since it invites disembodiment and dehumanization.

Spike Jonze's film *Her* (Ellison, Jonze, & Landay, 2013) about a man's romance with his operating system, received rave reviews and was touted as "prophetic" and "profound" (Generation Film, 2013). Similarly, *Ex Machina* (MacDonald, Reich, & Garland, 2015) is a film about a man who very convincingly develops a romantic interest in an android. Person-to-person contact is increasingly being replaced with person-to-machine contact, and as machines become more intelligent and interactive, this trend will become more common (Knafo & Lo Bosco, 2017). In Japan, many men have already fallen in love with a digital girlfriend made by Nintendo on a dating sim game, Love Plus. One man even married "her" (Lah, 2009). Consider here the omnipotent feats of imagination one must engage in to transform a digital image into a flesh-and-blood wife.

The male heterosexual often needs a magic wand, for the one he possesses between his legs is all too vulnerable. He often fetishizes a woman's body parts (hair, breasts, buttocks, feet) or inanimate objects (lingerie, fur, hose, leather) to soften and blur the difference between the sexes. The body of the woman inherently threatens him; she has a vagina, an outside and an inside, breasts, hips, curves, and softness he is drawn to but does not understand. She is an erotic landscape whose origin is maternal, a constellation of small infinities. Approaching her all at once is too frightening, for she threatens impotence and even castration. To deal with this potentially traumatic reality, he might ask her to wear special clothing – leather, pantyhose, or jewelry. He may want to focus his attention on a particular body part, thereby building a bridge to her totality and rendering her approachable. He might fetishize a high-heeled shoe, lending the woman a symbolic phallus, which serves as a lucky charm both to alleviate his castration anxiety (she too has a penis – albeit a symbolic one) or homophobia (although phallic, she's still a woman), and to make her genitals acceptable for sex. This strategy may be largely unconscious, a defense against the fear of impotence and castration. But for the devoted fetishist, this transformation is transcendent, and his devout worship of the object is nothing less than a sacred act and even a magical one.

Whatever the perversion, it rides on a fantasy of overcoming fear, pain, loss, and death and finding a paradise of transcendence, wholeness, and perfection. This impossible quest has vast social implications, since it can lead to a quest for a grand utopia that often results in hellish realms fostering oppression, persecution, and mass murder. The fantasy of being all-powerful, of being able to wish the impossible into existence, brings into the world both wonderful creations and devastating destruction.

Sexuality and creativity

When people conjure images of humans engaging in sexual activity, they imagine naked bodies fondling each other, groaning and sweating, as they gratify their biological needs and primal lust. Sometimes these behaviors are considered the most intimate and loving acts possible for humans. At other times, they are seen as forbidden, hidden, compulsive, or perverse. Perhaps no image is more emblematic of the human animal's body than the image of sexuality.

When summoning images of artists, people envision a very different picture: painters, paintbrush in hand, forming images on their canvases; composers writing down the notes to express the music in their minds; writers at a computer or with pen and pad in hand, weaving narratives from life and imagination. These acts are believed to represent the most sublime of human possibilities. Whereas sexuality seems primal, connecting people to their animal bodies, creativity engages the mind at its most elevated and inspirational level. What can these two human activities – art and sex – possibly have in common? As already mentioned, Eros is largely driven by the mind, so both activities are mind-driven. Both sex and creativity are also highly cathected activities that totally engage those involved, sometimes even compulsively and addictively. Thus, both activities can be overwhelming, leading some to feel out of control. Both activities can get blocked. Artists experience creative blocks and people's sexuality often becomes frozen and inhibited. Both acts are loaded with personal and cultural symbolism, communicated both consciously and unconsciously. Indeed, creativity and sexuality reveal how people think about themselves and relate to others. Those involved – the sexual beings or the artists – are frequently the last to know what really drives them.

Certainly, sexuality and creativity both carry omnipotent wishes, as they connect us to our life force and use libido to make something out of nothing: birth of a child, birth of a lived fantasy, birth of artistic expression, and birth of new ideas. But both activities force people to grapple with death and issues of mortality, as they are an insurgence against nature's finality. Chasseguet-Smirguel (1984) noted similarities between perversion and creativity, emphasizing the common need to create in both processes. Yet she claimed that whereas the artist sublimates, the pervert idealizes. Naturally, sublimation and idealization can co-occur.

More interesting than direct comparisons are the ways in which creativity can represent a transformation of sexuality. Freud was the first to write about creativity as a sublimation of sexuality, indicating that it was the highest form one's sexuality could assume. Freud (1905/1953, p. 50) noted:

> Perversions are neither bestial nor degenerate in the emotional sense of the word. They are the development of germs, all of which are contained in the undifferentiated sexual dispositions of the child, and which, by being suppressed or by being diverted to higher, asexual aims – by being sublimated – are destined to provide the energy for a great
> number of our cultural achievements.

Perversion also springs from a creative act, an encounter with a limit that invites and even demands crossing. At the benign and innovative end of the spectrum, perversion can generate creative possibilities. In transgressing against the norm and shattering sexual and social limits, the perverse violation can result in new cultural forms in art, philosophy, social relations, politics, science, and technology. Technology is itself a clear illustration of the perverse generative possibility (Knafo & Lo Bosco, 2017). Alfred Hitchcock is an example of an artist in whom creativity and perversion crossed paths. In a conversation with fellow filmmaker François Truffaut, he admitted being sexually celibate but using his films as an outlet for his sexual fantasies (Kirby, 1999). Hitchcock's fantasies were clearly sadistic, and his biographer claimed that he had a strong "association between sex and murder, between ecstasy and death" (p. 91) – an association that he had actors play out in his films. He "filmed scenes of murder as if they were love scenes and love scenes as if they were murder scenes" (Spoto, 1983, p. 331) His sadism toward women – usually beautiful blondes – involved a transference based on his intense attachment to his mother. He controlled the performance of actresses in minute detail and is known to have said, "The trouble today is that we don't torture the women enough" (p. 458). Tippi Hedren, star of *The Birds* and *Marnie*, claimed in her 2016 autobiography that Hitchcock harassed and stalked her. "It was sexual. It was perverse, and it was ugly," she wrote (Hedren, 2016, p. 72). Yet Hitchcock is repeatedly cited as one of the top directors of all time, and usually the number-one director of the film noir genre (Spoto, 1983).

Sexuality and creativity are familiar bedfellows in the lives of other artists as well. Mick Jagger, lead singer and songwriter of the Rolling Stones, is known to have an unrivaled sexual appetite; his biographer (Andersen, 2012) claimed he bedded more than 4,000 women and men, young and old. His sexuality found expression in his music and lyrics as well as in his relationship to his audiences. "What I'm doing is a sexual thing," he explained, referring to the way he seductively pranced around the stage (p. 64). The Rolling Stones logo – thick sensual lips with a protruding tongue – was Jagger's idea. *The New Yorker* magazine once compared the recognizability of Jagger's mouth to McDonald's golden arches (Norman, 2012, p. 594).

While married to Jerry Hall, who considered him to be a sex addict, Jagger agreed to see a sex therapist but ended up seducing her. Natasha Terry, the therapist, later referred to Jagger as a "sex vampire." According to Andersen (2012), Jagger most enjoyed seducing women who looked like him (e.g. Carly Simon, Bianca Jagger), indicating a narcissistic cast to his sexual preferences. He also liked seducing women who were partnered with other men. Apparently, he seduced Brian Jones's ex, and then Brian Jones himself, creating a bisexual triangle (Andersen, 2012). As of 2016, 72-year-old Jagger and his 29-year-old girlfriend became parents, he to his eighth child.

Georges Simenon was an extremely prolific writer, publishing 425 books, some of them under pseudonyms, including the famous series of Commissaire Maigret. His second wife claimed he had sex with over a thousand women, though he estimated the number was as high as 10,000, which included 8,000 prostitutes. Simenon said he had sex for the same reason he wrote: because he had an unsatisfied hunger for human contact, what he called "a devouring hunger for women" (Marnham, 1992, p. 160). Indeed, his sexual escapades and creativity became intimately linked, as both were compulsive, and many of the women he slept with became characters in his fiction. Marnham (1992) described Simenon's cold and critical mother who left Simenon feeling rejected and unloved. His insatiable sexual hunger and his need for female contact seem to have been the way he soothed that wound and fueled his writing. When Simenon lived in Paris, he had sex every day, frequently sleeping with four women each day, and every few months he'd indulge in a "frenzied orgy of work" (Currey, 2013, p. 231). He'd "write a novel with the same sudden, violent energy with which he made love, his books frequently ending in psychic explosion – a murder, a suicide or some other doom" (Marnham, 1992, p.163).

Picasso is also known to have linked sexuality and art. Indeed, women were very central to Picasso's life and creativity. His oeuvre is replete with idealized and denigrated images of the women he loved. Picasso grew up among women who adored him; his mother, sisters, and aunts lavished him with attention and affection. He did not wish to be like his father who, in his eyes, was submissive to the needs of his wife. Picasso therefore became the narcissistic, powerful, and dominant exploiter of women. His first sexual experience took place at the age of 13 with a prostitute. After that, he was never alone because he transitioned from one relationship to another, often continuing the older relationship while the new one took off. Peter Schjeldahl (2001) claimed Picasso made love the way he made art, "with domineering audacity and gloating pride" (2001). His biographer John Richardson said:

> Picasso loved, loved like a madman, furiously seeking the woman who would feed his art, his life, his dream of eternity … to draw from her inspiration and creativity, which he exhausted before ineluctably abandoning her and recommencing the same game with another woman – and then another.
> (Richardson in Pressman 2011, p. 24)

Picasso identified with the Minotaur, a mythological creature that frequently appears in his art: the bull-man to whom maidens are served and sacrificed.

Whereas Gustav Flaubert abstained from sex because he felt humiliated by it and believed it would siphon off his creative energies (Wall, 2001), Honoré de Balzac masturbated to the edge of orgasm and wrote in that state of frenzy (Currey, 2013). John Cheever believed that sex improved his creativity and even his eyesight (Currey, 2013). Thomas Wolfe one day accidentally discovered that touching his genitals increased his inspiration and motivation to write. After that, he used this method regularly to stoke his creative energy (Donald, 1987).

Anaïs Nin, who became famous for her erotic diaries, was beaten as a child and called ugly by her larger-than-life father. The only time he showed his affection was when he took naked photos of her. Nin believed she was the reason her father abandoned his family, and she began writing her famous diary as a way of "creating for herself, in words, a 'good girl,' one worthy of love, to replace the bad girl who had been rejected by Papa" (Fitch, 1993, p. 4). Caught between her Catholic upbringing and intense sensuality, Nin masturbated compulsively and flirted with men shamelessly, engaging in sexually compulsive behavior. She seduced many men and women, including several father figures – two of her analysts – and later used them as inspirations for her writing. At the age of 30, she even engaged in a sexual marathon with her father (Nin, 1969). Her diary writing became as compulsive as her need for sex. When Otto Rank, her second analyst, asked her to stop writing in her diary, she replied that "this was as difficult as asking a drug addict to do without drugs" (Nin, 1966, p. 280).

The sexual illusionist

Sexuality and creativity arise from the human condition, while perversions exemplify T. S. Eliot's statement that humans cannot tolerate very much reality (Eliot, 1963, p. 190). This is why a person acting out a perversion can be called a *sexual illusionist*, one who devises creative but sometimes highly tricky solutions to life's problems. A key reason perversions fascinate us is that they mirror our own need to master trauma, take revenge, transcend limitations, and manage what might easily overwhelm us. Trauma is part of everyone's life, and even the most fortunate do not escape loss, sickness, old age, and death. Life makes even the most "normal" among us more than a little crazy. When we better understand how perversion comes into being and engages life, we can begin to appreciate its aspects of creativity and humanity and what it says about the psychological and existential situations common to all people.

Everyone creates illusions to help them live and does a bit of magic in the service of self-deception. Everyone objectifies others, retreats from life, and dulls their own sentience to some degree. We all suffer and create unconscious strategies to manage our pain and fear. There are some things we simply don't want to know, no matter how much we love the truth. Nearly everyone takes the break that some perverse activity grants. But most people do not feel the need to adhere to a rigid script that must be endlessly repeated in exactly the same way. In the case of perversion proper, the magic show never ends.

Chapter 2

Elixirs of immortality

Transformations of intoxication

> There are two states in which man arrives at the rapturous feeling of existence, namely in dreaming and in intoxication.
>
> Nietzsche, 1870/2013

Clinicians regularly encounter "drug magic" in their work with patients while guiding their process of articulating the complex experiences of addiction. When listening carefully, they can hear the omnipotent fantasies in verbalizations of the experiences of compulsive drug users. In the early stages of addiction, the user sees the world as a magical fantasyland rather than a foreboding reality. Consider the "head shop" that sells drug paraphernalia, decorated with black lights, psychedelic artwork, and lava lamps, their colors dancing in slow motion. The glass-blown bowls, water pipes, and bongs feature prominent magic mushrooms, the faces of popular cartoon characters, superheroes, or fantastical animal illustrations. Additionally, marijuana "edibles" take the form of sugary delicacies such as brownies, cupcakes, gummy bears, and chocolates, treats that usually appeal more to children than adults.

Drugs alter experience. After downing a few shots of bourbon, the world takes on a hazy, dreamlike quality, and the drinker achieves the desired emotional distance from his most troublesome problems. This is called "taking the edge off." A few hits of marijuana can remove the armor of social propriety and get the user "out of their head." A few bumps of cocaine can lift the iron blanket off a mind-numbing depression. This is called "getting up." The idioms referring to the effects of intoxication suggest why drug use and recidivism continue to increase. Quite simply put, drugs work as intended, and that's why treatment is difficult. They offer something many people want, need, or are missing – they make people feel good. The problem arises when drugs stop working, when the euphoria lessens and the misery of the "come down" increases. In this regard, omnipotent fantasies can serve to perpetuate addictive behaviors, promising the impossible: earlier states of euphoria and the continued successful flight from painful truths.

The search for a magical solution to life's problems, a "fix" based on a dream of mastery over self and world, originates from and feeds omnipotent fantasy. A magic potion, a panacea, a genie in a bottle, or a needle – who would not want one? Without the throbbing desire to transform what might otherwise seem unalterable, who would synthesize and consume psychoactive substances? Without the capacity to dream and desire, who would pursue intoxication? Why cultivate strands of cannabis, extract cocaine from the leaves of the coca plant? Why manufacture, smuggle, and distribute illegal drugs? Why manufacture and use tobacco and alcohol? Why plant two Starbucks stores within a half-mile of each other? The simple answer is because the human condition is so painful. Because it needs a *fix*. This is what technology does or at least hopes to do, and this is what drugs promise. Drugs don't simply change *how* we think or feel; they also change *who we are*. They change our relationships. We think, feel, and act differently under the influence, inhabit an altered reality, relate to altered people. If use becomes chronic, the relationship to self and other refers first to the user's relationship with the drug. Indeed, the drug itself can become the significant other in people's lives. They wake up thinking about it, organize their day around using it, make plans to keep themselves supplied with it, and anticipate feeling its effects the way others might anticipate the experience of intimacy.

Drugs can create the illusion of omnipotence and crush the user in the same day or even the same hour. While drugs gratify needs and grant life-changing experiences, they also create the need for more and then just a little more. The charm and enchantment thin as the downward spiral begins, and the dream of more is replaced by the reality of abuse. As people become emotionally unavailable and physically compromised, they become slaves of compulsion. Gollum, a compelling character in J. R. R. Tolkien's *Lord of the Rings* trilogy, is obsessed with the ring of power he carries, but it eventually twists his body and mind, and almost destroys him, an apt representation of the chronic user's relationship with a drug. The drug becomes teacher, lover, friend, purpose, and eventually enemy, and perhaps even executioner. Furthermore, as in relationships with lovers, breakups can be extremely painful. Recovering addicts routinely admit at Alcoholics Anonymous and Narcotics Anonymous meetings how much they miss their old friends – their substances of choice. That is because drugs not only fulfill omnipotent fantasies, but also defend against existential anxiety associated with mortality. Additionally, drugs can offer an experience or process that was missing from early life, such as the states of omnipotence contained in what Winnicott (1945) called the "holding environment."

Limitless

People have long used psychoactive substances to escape the frightening existential realities of the human condition and mortality (Becker, 1973; Fromm, 1956/2006). Becker was among the first to develop a robust theory implicating addiction in humankind's denial of death, but others have followed him in describing omnipotent wish fulfillment as a means to transcend human limitations. Dodes (1990) added layers of theoretical texture in his work on drug abuse, claiming that addiction is powered by omnipotent fantasies of magically reversing intolerable human feelings of helplessness. He wrote about the association between drug abuse and "narcissistic rage," manifesting in the experience of human limitation and the need to "re-establish a sense of power" (p. 398). For Dodes, drugs restore a sense of omnipotence by granting the user the power to manipulate the forces of the world – both internal and external. As journalist and recovering heroin addict Ann Marlowe (1999) said, "Addiction creates a god so that time will stop – why all gods are created" (pp. 155–156). In her memoir, *How to Stop Time: Heroin from A to Z*, Marlowe offers a raw, human portrayal of the magical fantasies that initially drove her heroin use and chronic relapses on her road to recovery. She poignantly describes heroin's power to create the illusion of asserting omnipotent control over the world, including fantasies of wielding power over the forces of time and being able to reverse the aging process. For her, addiction is a battle enlisted to fill in the deepest holes of human needs and to conquer feelings of powerlessness (Marlowe, 1999).

Contemporary American culture continues to tout the ability of drugs to silence intimations of mortality. Consider, for instance, the appeal of the 2011 film *Limitless* (Dixon, Kroopf, & Kavanaugh, 2011). The film starred Bradley Cooper as Eddie Morra, a struggling writer who drinks too much and can't keep a relationship together or meet a deadline. Eddie's life was essentially in shambles until he happened upon NZT – a government top-secret nootropic (smart drug enhancing cognition) that activated regions of his brain allowing him to achieve far beyond the reaches of his comparatively impotent form – instantly transforming him into a super-human productivity machine by merely popping a pill. The movie depicted Eddie Morra's conquests over the rest of the merely mortal human race as he effortlessly overcame all adversities to take the world by storm, obtaining money, power, and women. The film was so well received that it spawned a 2015 television series adaptation with the same name.

Eddie Morra is not the only one searching for magical solutions. Researchers have estimated that, as of 2014, approximately 30 percent of college students – particularly those who attend highly competitive colleges – use pharmaceutical stimulants such as Adderall, Concerta, Vyvanse, and Dexedrine as performance-enhancing "study drugs" (Yanes, 2014). The demand for these "smart drugs," which were formulated to treat attention deficit hyperactivity disorder (ADHD), increased so quickly that pharmacies ran out; a shortage of the medications occurred in 2011–2012 (NIDA Notes, 2014). In response to the shortage, the U.S. Drug Enforcement Agency raised the quota for production, illustrating the magnitude of the rise of prescriptions written for psychostimulants over the past decade (NIDA Notes, 2014). According to a study conducted by the National Institutes of Health (NIH) and the Agency for Healthcare Research and Quality (AHRQ) (Zuvekas, Vitiello, & Norquist, 2012), the use of prescription psychostimulants increased significantly, going from a prevalence rate among youth of 0.6

percent in 1987 to 2.9 percent in 2002. Recent reports suggested that the prescribed use of these medications for the diagnosis of ADHD has continued to rise. Based on the Health Resources and Services Administration's National Survey of Children's Health, the percentage of children age 4–17 years diagnosed with ADHD increased from 7.8 percent in 2003 to 9.5 percent (Centers for Disease Control and Prevention, 2007, pp. 1439–1443). The National Institute of Mental Health (NIMH) estimated that about 60 percent of children with ADHD are treated with medication (Zuvekas, Vitiello, & Norquist, 2012). These researchers also found a steadily increasing growth rate in the prescription of these drugs between 1987 and 1996 of about 17 percent per year (Zuvekas, Vitiello, & Norquist, 2012). The rise in "smart drug" use and abuse highlights the dissatisfaction our culture has with limitation and finitude. Better, stronger, and longer has always held a universal appeal, yet some are more easily enchanted by magic than others. And for those addicted to magic, childhood plays a large role in what they might be missing and what the drug offers as a substitute. In any case, such inquiry leads us back home, to the "holding environment."

The moment of inebriation

As mentioned above, drugs transform experience of self and other. While not specifically addressing addiction problems, Winnicott furthered understanding of omnipotent fantasies in relation to self-development. In his landmark concept of the "holding environment," Winnicott (1945) proposed that there are moments when infants exist in a state of complete and total satiation – a magical experience where, for that moment, the biological and psychological needs of the infant are no longer impinging upon its awareness. He described this "moment of illusion," as a state of bathing in "subjective omnipotence" (p. 141). For Winnicott, the caregiver who is attuned and dedicated to gratifying the immediate needs of the infant fosters the infant's experience of itself as the all-powerful center of the universe, embracing omnipotent fantasies of being the sole "creator of the world" and gratifier of its own needs. For the infant in this very early stage of psychic development, there is no separate other providing nurturance, satiation, and protection from the outside world. Thus, we can only imagine the narcissistic injury incurred through the process of learning that one is *not* the all-powerful center of being. Winnicott (1971) suggested that those who cannot tolerate the withdrawal of infantile omnipotence due to a particularly abrupt suspension of this experience lack a normal sense of existing in the world as "real" people.

Winnicott's theories inspired and informed a number of contemporary psychoanalytic perspectives on addiction (Bollas, 1987; Director, 2002; Ulman & Paul, 2006) – in particular, those theories that highlight how drugs provide a magical experience similar to Winnicott's (1945) satiated infant experience as the "moment of illusion" (p. 141). In his reimagining of

Winnicott's (1971) ideas regarding illusions and reality in the context of the caregiver–child relationship, Bollas (1987) proposed that compulsive drug-seeking behaviors in adult life can serve as a re-enactment of the search for a "transformational object," which he described as an archaic experience associated with intense affect and a metamorphosis of self (p. 14). He asserted that we seek experiences throughout life that we fantasize will transform us and the world (Bollas, 1987). Bollas suggested that such examples of the search for the transformational object include the expectation that another drink or one more hand of blackjack or an exciting sexual encounter will transform the self to a state closer to meeting one's needs. Charles Bukowski (1993/2003) was a writer who eloquently conveyed the function of alcohol in providing him with a makeshift bridge to attaining what Bollas described as a magical transformation of self. Bukowski wrote poignantly about alcohol's role in changing his experience of himself. In his poem, "The Bluebird," Bukowski grapples with a conflict between an authentic sense of himself versus that persona he feels he must present in the outside world to keep his vulnerable parts safe and protected. In this short poem, he reflects on his efforts to protect his "true" self (i.e. the bluebird) through the use of substances, which act as a wall behind which he can drown out the human songs desperate to be free (Bukowski, 1993/2003, p. 496).

Wurmser (1978/1995) characterized the cycle of compulsive drug use as a process set in motion by a narcissistic crisis, a self-shattering that brings fear and sorrow over which the user attempts to exert omnipotent control – "taking magical, omnipotent control over the uncontrollable" (p. 146). Wurmser suggested that these unbearable emotional states give way to "a longing, a frantic search for excitement and relief, a sense of aimless, intolerable restlessness, and craving" (p. 109). For those who feel "uncomfortable in their own skin," deeply unhappy, or enraged by their own experience, a substance can provide the portal through which another self can be imagined and magically embodied. Caroline Knapp's memoir provides innumerable personal articulations of a fantasy life wherein transformations of self are magically rendered by alcohol. In *Drinking: A Love Story* (1996), she recounts how alcohol granted her the permeability to merge with new, different personalities and more preferred versions of her self (p. 65).

In the theories already discussed, the process of transformation is the common thread that holds great significance for the user. For instance, Bollas's (1987) theory suggests that the drug is experienced as providing the process that brings about transformation rather than being the instrument of transformation itself. Thus, individuals searching for these early transformational processes discover that drugs can deliver a makeshift version of those missed experiences, but they don't necessarily see the drug itself as a surrogate or replacement caregiver. The relationship between the user and the drug itself is not the central focus of these theories. At the same time, the literature supports conceptualizations that do specifically address parallels in the relationship between the user and the drug and that of other relational patterns in the user's life (Bollas, 1987; Director, 2005; Ullman & Paul, 2006). For instance, many theories underline the adhesiveness of bonds to early representations of significant others in the psyche of addicted individuals. Addicted users may seek drugs to recreate a lost, yearned-for attachment. Some discover that, with drugs, they can create a profoundly comforting and powerful relational experience, the likes of which they have never felt.

The relational world of addiction

Perhaps just as powerful as the omnipotent strivings to overcome human limitations and shatter the boundaries of experience of self is the need to magically reverse or change relational patterns and the associated feelings of shame, deficiency, deprivation, imprisonment, or aloneness. While ostensibly a far cry from drive-model approaches to addictions, relational psychoanalytic perspectives of substance abuse find their roots in ideas first proposed by Freud and some of his early followers. Although Freud did not develop a comprehensive theory of substance abuse, he did suggest that problems of addiction primarily involve a displacement of infantile drives. In a letter to Wilhelm Fleiss, Freud cited masturbation as the "primary addiction" (1897/1950, p. 272):

> The insight has dawned on me that masturbation is the one major habit, the "primal addiction," and it is only as a substitute and replacement for it that the other addictions – to alcohol, morphine, tobacco and the like – come into existence.
>
> (Freud, 1897/1950, p. 272)

Fenichel (1945/1996) was the first of Freud's followers to add further depth to the picture of addictions as drive derivatives. Fenichel saw addiction as a mental state that becomes more oriented to omnipotent fantasies than to the realities of the external world. He proposed that drug addicts use the effects of alcohol and drugs

> to satisfy the archaic oral longing which is sexual longing, a need for security, and a need for the maintenance of self-esteem simultaneously … They are fixated to a passive-narcissistic aim and are interested solely in getting their gratification … Interests in reality gradually disappear, except those having to do with procuring the drug. In the end, all of reality may come to reside in the hypodermic needle. The tendency toward such a development, rooted in an oral dependence on outer supplies, is the essence of drug addiction.
>
> (Fenichel, 1945/1996, p. 376)

The implication of the theories of Freud and Fenichel is that addicted drug users become focused on the substance as a means to the end of instinctual need gratification, a replacement or substitute for the archaic oral need that continues to seek satisfaction. Many addiction theories that followed continued to see the drug as a substitute for something else; however, theorists began to consider the drug as a replacement for the loss or absence of significant others in the user's early relational world. For instance, Kohut (1977/2009a) viewed the drug user as someone seeking a "substitute for a self-object" (p. vii). According to his approach, drug users relate to people as if they are drugs, as existing purely to quell their emotional needs. They inhabit an enchanted wonderland wherein drugs and people are the magic potions that instantly silence the stinging, archaic echoes of abusive, depriving, or absentee caregiver relationships.

Further, a drug can serve as the missing piece that allows a person to feel whole, to experience a magical sense of merger or fusion with another – a process of two becoming one. Fromm (1956/2006) argued that, as self-aware beings, we are constantly striving to shield ourselves from the cold, ever-present truth that we are ultimately and utterly alone. Fromm proposed that a vast number of mental health problems, including drug addiction and other compulsions, are driven by efforts to overcome dreaded feelings of aloneness, by chasing after omnipotent fantasies of fusing with external objects. He believed that individuals attribute magical properties to objects in the external world, and life becomes organized around fantasies of ingesting the magical "other."

Since Fromm, the idea of omnipotent fantasies materializing in response to derailed or unresponsive primary relationships has been repeatedly stressed in formulations of the precipitation and perpetuation of cycles of compulsive drug use (Seinfeld, 1991; Wurmser, 1978/1995). For instance, Seinfeld (1991) regarded drug-seeking behaviors as a search for "nonhuman substitutes for human relationships" (p. 101). At the core of his formulation of chronic drug use is Fairbairn's (1952) theory regarding the human need to maintain ties to object representations in the internal world. Fairbairn asserted that individuals who experience deprivation in early relationships often develop a hyperactive dependency on and attachment to caregivers. Such extreme devotion to "bad" internalized caregivers exceeds that in healthy relationships characterized by reciprocal love (Fairbairn, 1952). In fact, human strivings for security, love, and connection grow even stronger in the face of threats to their gratification.

Fairbairn aimed to account for people who repeatedly seek out experiences that cause them pain – what Freud (1920/1955a) referred to as "repetition compulsion." Based on this same premise, Seinfeld conceptualized substance abuse as the impassioned pursuit of an inner bond with an exciting, rejecting object. For Seinfeld, compulsive drug use is an attempt to "fill the inner void of failed object relations" (1991, p. 104). In the wake of disappointing and depriving early relationships, the biological need for human relatedness engenders a "state of emptiness" that becomes the core of psychic structure

(Seinfeld, 1991). Seinfeld referred to this as "the empty core," which is experienced by the individual as a hunger directed internally and externally in a search to fill a sense of lacking or incompleteness. He proposed that it is the empty core that addicts seek to magically fill through compulsive consumption of chemicals, food, or sex.

Seinfeld's (1991) theory of the empty core has been enriched by the words of creative writer and alcoholic William Styron. Styron (1990) described alcohol as a "friend whose ministrations [he] sought daily ... as a means to calm the anxiety and incipient dread that [he] had hidden away for so long somewhere in the dungeons of [his] spirit" (p. 40). After giving up alcohol, Styron (1990) stated that he suffered a painful emotional void from deep within. "The comforting friend had abandoned me," he lamented (p. 41). He suggested that the feelings of "deprivation" engendered by his newfound sobriety were a "traumatic" event that marked the "onset of depressive mood" (Styron, 1990, p. 41, as cited in Wanamaker, 1999). In his memoir *Darkness Visible: A Memoir of Madness* (1990), he depicted the ways in which tragic childhood loss figured in the development and progression of his alcoholism. Alcohol is like a warm compress over a body that ached with loss and painful fears of abandonment.

In the same vein, Bukowski (1993/2003) once talked about the way his behavior and personality dramatically shifted when he drank too much. He speculated that he had internalized the "badness" of his father, reporting that on occasions when he experienced the most terrible drunken rages, he identified with the anger and meanness he had witnessed during childhood at the hands of his father. After describing his father as a coward and a bully, Bukowski was aware of loathing the part of himself that he recognized as his father (Markow, McCormick, & Dullaghan, 2003).

In "Son of Satan," Bukowski (1993/2003) wrote that his father once screamed at him: "I'm going to give you the beating of your life! I'm going to cure you! I'm not going to raise a son who is not fit for human society!" (p. 35). Although alcohol may have filled the role of an intimate companion or remedy for assuaging a painful sense of dread at times, Bukowski was also somewhat aware of his hunger for the abusive quality – both physically and emotionally – embodied in the drug. In an interview with *London Magazine*, Bukowski described his relationship with alcohol in a way that is hauntingly congruent with his description of the relationship he had with his father:

> Drinking is a form of suicide where you're allowed to return to life and begin all over the next day. It's like killing yourself, and then you're reborn.
>
> (Wennersten, 1975, pp. 49–50)

Like Seinfeld, Tatarsky (2002) described the addictive relationship as a re-enactment of the pursuit to maintain ties to an early internal object. He placed particular emphasis on the nature of the drug as a representation of what Fairbairn (1952) called the "exciting object." The drug becomes the focus of the individual's desire to address needs and feelings that are never fully acknowledged. Tatarsky (2002) regarded addiction as a distraction that keep the individual's focus away from seeking real solutions to deeper unfulfilled needs. In the compulsion to use an addictive substance, there is a denial of the existence of the actual problem that needs addressing. This form of denial may temporarily act as a protective shield against the individual's awareness of building anxiety conjured up by echoes of the deeper need. The real need underlying a psychological or physiological addiction to a substance is never met because the individual is caught up in pursuing a drug, fantasy, or symbolic solution that only satisfies the surface need. As a result, the deeper need grows in intensity, and this continues to perpetuate the addictive search (Tatarsky, 2002). Wurmser (1978/1995) also suggested that the relationship between the user and the drug can mirror the early childhood dynamics of dependency that develop in the child's efforts to establish and maintain contact with an early caregiver who has tantalized the individual with love, only to withdraw this coveted object before the child is gratified.

Director (2002) proposed that underlying most compulsive drug use and its physiological components is "a relational impasse that finds concrete expression in the act of drug use, that, in turn, sustains it" (p. 551). She suggested that chronic drug use achieves its power over the addict because it captures dynamics that derive from unresolved early relational matrices. In other words, the drug itself becomes a "decoy" for a self-defeating, repetitive tie to an earlier relationship. For instance, drug use can be unconsciously driven by unresolved conflicts in relational patterns, such as dependency and defiance, domination and submission, or sacrifice and greed. Rather than face these conflicts in their relationships with real people, the user forms relationships with substances that come to represent "stand-ins" for those people. Through the rituals of their addiction, the user repeats unconscious relational patterns (Director, 2002, p. 556).

Similarly, Wurmser (1978/1995) pointed out that many addicts describe their drug and the associated rituals of use with a tenderness that echoes narratives about human love partners:

> The very phrase drug dependency reminds us of what we are dealing with, namely an archaic passive dependency on an all-giving, hugely inflated object, as evident in the single-minded devotedness and frenzy of the chase after the beloved, in the incorporative greed, the masturbatory and orgiastic aspects of the use, and the mixture of ecstatic idealization and deprecation vis-à-vis the drug ("star dust," "blue heavens," "white lady" versus "shit," "scag") … Far beyond dependency on the drug, there exists a deep passive dependency on others, often quite impersonal others.
> (Wurmser, 1978/1995, pp. 160–161)

In her powerful memoir of heroin addiction, Marlowe (1999) describes her relationship with heroin as unfolding with a frighteningly familiar congruence to her relationships with romantic partners: "Past the first thrill, dope use is mainly a power struggle, which the user always loses. If you feel that this is what romance is about, addiction can easily look like a love affair" (p. 256). The notion of the drug as lover is further expressed by the self-identified alcoholic writer Caroline Knapp (1996), who compared the progression of her relationship with alcohol to the deterioration of a romantic relationship:

> When you love somebody, or something, it's amazing how willing you are to overlook the flaws ... I started to dry-heave in the mornings, driving to work in my car. A tremor in my hands developed, then grew worse, then persisted for longer periods, all day sometimes. I did my best to ignore all this. I struggled to ignore it, the way a woman hears coldness in a lover's voice and struggles, mightily and knowingly, to misread it.
>
> (p. 10)

The power of psychoactive chemicals have enchanted, tantalized, and disenfranchised humankind since the beginning of time. Similar to the magic dust often sprinkled over an individual when that person becomes the love object of another, the "high" produced by a drug can elicit experiences of deep peace and perfection. For the individual in love, an ordinary, flawed human being can be transformed into a godlike, perfect figure. This idealization of a lover is analogous to that of the user in the honeymoon phase of a drug addiction. Through the use of a euphoric drug, one can unleash the power to fill their body from head to toe with the enchanting warmth of a lover's embrace. On the other hand, as the relationship unfolds, certain realities set in and the idealization gradually begins to fade, the process of addiction can turn a drug against its user, stamping on their heart and ultimately delivering profound emotional deprivation and loss. In many such cases, the fantasies that accompany the psychoactive effects of intoxicating substances cast a dreadful spell on its users – a spell that feels irreversible for the addicted individual, leaving them to toil in utter powerlessness.

Chapter 3

Mightier than the sword

The magic of creativity

> We do not need magic to transform our world. We carry all of the power we
> need inside ourselves.
>
> J. K. Rowling (2011)

Little debate in psychoanalysis exists about the centrality of omnipotent fantasies in creative processes. Omnipotent fantasies are sublimated in creative urges that endeavor to change ourselves, the significant others in our lives, and the world around us (Becker, 1973; Freud, 1909/1955b; Kohut, 1977/2009b; Rank, 1932/1989; Winnicott, 1971). We retain the residues of these fantasies, originally derived from infancy, and mobilize them in countless efforts to express and work through our subjective experiences. In this chapter, we explore how these archaic fantasies achieve materialization through human acts of creativity.

Immortality in creativity

Writers, especially those who produce fiction, can create worlds that enable catharsis and relief from a reality that seems indifferent and without inherent meaning. Freud (1908/1986) suggested that "every child at play behaves like an imaginative writer, in that he creates a world of his own or, more truly, he rearranges the things of his world and orders it in a new way that pleases him better" (p. 45). Freud believed that, as adults, we retain some remnant of the narcissistic illusions of infancy once allowing us to exist as omnipotent beings. He asserted that children's play is transferred to the adult form of "play" in the expression of art: "The creative writer does the same as a child at play. He creates a world of phantasy which he takes very seriously – that is, which he invests with large amounts of emotion – while separating it sharply from reality" (p. 144). Freud (1913/1961c) believed that artists fashioned alternate realities:

> The artist's first aim is to set himself free and, by communicating his work
> to other people suffering from the same arrested desires, he offers them

the same liberation ... Art is a conventionally accepted reality in which, thanks to artistic illusion, symbols and substitutes are able to provoke real emotions. Thus art constitutes a region half-way between a reality which frustrates wishes and the wish-fulfilling world of the imagination – a region in which, as it were, primitive man's strivings for omnipotence are still in full force.

(pp. 187–188)

Numerous theorists and creative writers have deepened the existential premises of Freud's propositions about the functions of narcissistic illusions. Many have characterized creativity as a process that enables an artist to exhibit courage in the face of grim, mute – mortal – reality (Becker, 1973; Freud, 1920/1955a; Kohut, 1977/2009b; Rank, 1932/1989; Winnicott, 1971). For instance, in *Art and the Artist*, Rank (1932/1989) underscored the acute sensitivity of the artist to the existential dilemma, saying that conventional illusions such as art and religion are not enough; one also needs one's inner illusions of omnipotence. Creative vitality itself can serve a protective function, providing shelter from the frightening awareness of our vulnerabilities. Becker extended Rank's ideas to his treatment of the various defense mechanisms by which humans shield themselves from mortal reality, suggesting the production of art was a triumph of sorts over mortality and death. In a collection of essays titled *The Inevitable: Contemporary Writers Confront Death*, American novelist David Foster Wallace articulated a similar sentiment:

I strongly suspect a big part of [a writer's job] is to aggravate this sense of entrapment and loneliness and death in people, to move people to countenance it, since any possible human redemption requires us first to face what's dreadful, what we want to deny.

(Wallace as cited in Shields & Morrow, 2011, p. 12)

David Foster Wallace's creative denial only went so far; in the end he took his own life.

Recreating the world

In seeking to overcome the limitations of the human form, the creative scientist transforms the world of objects, including the human body, while artists create cathartic and liberating structures. For instance, Knafo (2012) recounts the story of a child who was locked in a room by himself for hours at a time by an abusive parent. Frightened and confused, he eventually discovered he did not *have to* remain within the confines of that room but could travel inward and inhabited a more palatable environment through the use of imagination and fantasy. As an adult, he became a novelist.

Winnicott (1945) regarded the omnipotent fantasies of the infant's internal world as the first creative act. He proposed that in the earliest months of infancy – a stage of primary narcissism – children fantasize they are meeting their own needs through their own sheer will. As noted in the previous chapter, in this "moment of illusion" the child is creating its world (p. 141). This moment will echo when, for instance, later in the child's life the parent loses a game to the child on purpose. Further on, as children grow and direct care is withdrawn, they will begin to feel autonomous – creatures possessing their own will and energies, self-contained, self-made, and self-determined. Of course, such clear-cut independence is an illusion but one necessary for the development of a sense of autonomy.

Winnicott believed children spend a great deal of time inhabiting a world in which they draw from the well of primary narcissism to promote a sense of existence as effective beings who possess the power to change themselves, others, and the world around them. Imaginary friends and fictional characters offer children the illusion of mastery and control over the world in a time when they are first coming to recognize an overwhelming sense of helplessness and vulnerability (Fraiberg, 1959). The playful act of hosting a tea party in a small circle of dolls and stuffed animals allows children to transform their subjective self-perceptions and assume, through identification, the role of parental figures with the power to lead a social event.

Children can become fanatics in their love and devotion to the superheroes they identify with; the bedroom walls become plastered with depictions of super-powerful beings, whose roles they live out in play. So much of what they treasure – toys, books, clothes, shows, and movies – reflects the need for healthy illusions that steel them against their vulnerability, aloneness, and helplessness. To survive intact, the child must create a world within a world that is smaller, safer, and controllable.

> For adults, play in the form of creative expression has its foundation in these childhood efforts to *create* the world in a more manageable form. If the adult creates a world even more terrifying than the real one, he or she is still in charge. Through narcissistic illusions, creative adults wield the power to mold subjective realities into the shape they *need* them to be (Bollas, 1987; Ehrenzweig, 1967; Kohut, 1977/2009b; Winnicott, 1971).

Bollas (1987) took Winnicott's ideas further in finding the mother's presence in primary narcissism as a "transformational object" – something that resembles more of a process than a separate identifiable other with its own subjective experience. For Bollas, the mother transmitted an "aesthetic of being" to her child that becomes a feature of the child's self. "As the infant's 'other' self, the mother transforms the baby's internal and external environment" (p. 13). He saw creativity as one part of the wide-ranging collective search in adult life for that long-lost object associated with the process of metamorphosis. Bollas said the "aesthetic space allows for a creative enactment of the search for this transformational object relation ... in the arts we have a location for ... intense memories of the process of self-transformation" (p. 29).

Ana Mendieta's art is a good example of such creative enactments. A Cuban-born artist torn from her mother and motherland at an early age, Mendieta later used her art to attempt to master the painful fissure of separation and loss. She created sculptural pieces called Siluetas that blend into the natural landscape. Although her art deals with loss and death, it exhibits a transformational power derived from the artistic gesture that breathes life into natural materials. Mendieta created a ritual that she repeated time and time again: creation, destruction, death, and regeneration.

For Mendieta, making art was a spiritual act. She saw herself as a dynamic conduit, the willing shaman who left a talisman to work its magic with the elements. An artist in exile, Mendieta claimed space after space only to create a powerfully felt absence within them. She reproduced her concrete form by shaping her silhouette into the earth; yet that very form, so fragile and delicate, susceptible to weather changes and the forces of nature, gradually vanished, leaving only a trace of what once existed. Mendieta's physical body became, in the end, a numinous presence. Although her art, like a child's sandcastle, was not protected against change and dissolution, its restoration was ironically guaranteed through its gracious return to and merger with the surround that furnished its existence (Knafo, 2009).

Others have expanded and enriched the vitality of theories about the origins of art by looking at the experiences of creative writers. For instance, Slochower (1998) proposed that narcissistic illusions serve the creative writer as temporary solutions to the anxieties that hinder creative processes. She credited the idealized illusions that inhabit the creative space with generating "moments of illusion" that protect the writer from being consumed by the inevitable "moments of failure" (Winnicott, 1945, p. 141). She said,

> the idealized illusion helps the writer largely to avoid self-doubt and anxiety, and to construct a temporary form of insulated space. That protected space allows the writer to enter the creative arena and to write with an illusion of intellectual power and certainty.
>
> (Slochower, 1998, p. 333)

Also keeping with Winnicott's (1971) ideas about omnipotent fantasies in infancy, Aron (1995) has reflected on his personal experience as a writer and psychoanalytic theoretician. He pointed to the acceptance of his own sense of grandiosity as critical in granting him the freedom to recreate the world in his thinking and writing. Aron suggested that the psychoanalytic writer must allow himself the fantasy of recasting, which may even consist of destroying the work of his analytic forefathers. Once this manic and implicitly defensive phase of the creative process has reached completion, the author then subjects his creative output to the reality testing characterized by "objective" judgment. Aron (1995) celebrated the writer's omnipotent fantasies of changing the world as a source of inspiration to be nurtured rather than overcome:

> I believe that it is only by allowing myself the grandiose phantasy that I can recreate that I can allow myself to begin to think through the issues involved in any one paper. Conflicts relating to the regulation of grandiosity are often responsible for the difficulty that so many analysts have in writing papers. To control these narcissistic conflicts it is tempting to inhibit one's grandiosity, and in eliminating access to one's omnipotent and omniscient phantasies, people deprive themselves of an important prerequisite to the creative process.
>
> (p. 196)

Writer Charles Bukowski believed his creativity gave him enormous power. Bukowski (1982) often described experiencing his existence in the world as inconsequential – especially when relating to his parents, friends, and women. Nonetheless, the response he engendered in others through his writing opened his mind to the potential he possessed for impacting the external world. In one autobiographical account, he recalled his first experience of literary potency when his teacher read his essay to the class to inspire other students.

> Everybody was listening. I drank in my words like a thirsty man. I even began to believe them ... All too soon it was over.
>
> (Bukowski, 1982, p. 43)

Bukowski found his magic, a way for his existence to have meaning in the world. In the following stanza, he described his fragmentation and its reversal through artistic expression:

> This man sometimes forgets who
> he is.
> sometimes he thinks he's the
> Pope.
> other times he thinks he's a
> hunted rabbit
> and hides under the
> bed.
> then
> all at once
> he'll recapture total
> clarity
> and begin creating
> works of
> art.
> (Bukowski, 1982, pp. 442–443)

Transformation of trauma

Psychoanalytic theorists have written about the power of art to transform traumatic experiences (Knafo, 2012; Richman, 2014). Indeed, at times art has been created to address trauma and/or face death, whether real or imagined, and involves an aesthetic response to human emergency (Stiles, 1992). In such cases, art represents an attempt to magically shift power relations by handing power to those most in need of safety and support. Paradoxically, although the content of this art may be destruction, its purpose is to prevent and relieve trauma, thus preserving the survivor's power to live, to be spontaneous, to fantasize, and to dream. This type of art is in the service of mastery over destruction, loss, numbing, and mourning.

An example of this kind of art is the work of Charlotte Salomon (1917–1943), a woman who experienced childhood trauma (a family history of multiple suicides) that assumed a new form in the context of an imposed social and political tragedy (Nazi persecution and genocide). Shortly before she was murdered in Auschwitz in 1943, when she was 26 and five months pregnant, Salomon completed a barely veiled autobiographical picture-novel and musical theater piece titled *Leben? oder Theater?* (Life? or Theater?) – a brave, life-affirming project that transcended the morbidity of its inspiration and content. Salomon crafted this amazing work of art because, in her words, "I have a feeling the whole world has to be put back together again" (Salomon, in Herzberg, 1981, p. 774). Rather than follow in the footsteps of the women in her family – her mother, grandmother, and aunt – all of whom had committed suicide, Salomon chose instead to transform her private trauma into a work of art, a work that has become a noble testament to the power of spiritual preservation (Knafo, 2009).

Although her work did not succeed in saving her life, it seems to have saved her spiritually, in that it recontextualized her existence in a form and meaning that transcended its tragic personal and social context. It allowed her to visit (and recreate with truth) her past, no matter how painful, in the context of a terrifying present and future. This work brought to life her youthful passion and creative spirit, connecting her, in her isolated, exiled state, to those most dear to her and breathing life back into the dead, in a blatant refusal to accept their disappearance from her life. With this work she battled the numbing forces of death, facing the truth about her family and the world and finding herself. She wrote:

> The war raged on and I sat by the sea and saw deep into the heart of humankind. I was my mother my grandmother indeed I was all the characters in the play. I learned to walk all paths and became myself.
>
> (Felstiner, 1994, p. 141)

Creativity and addiction

Many people expect creative individuals to abuse substances and are hardly surprised to discover that yet another famous artist has checked into a rehabilitation facility or died from a drug overdose. A *New York Times* op-ed piece (Mehlman, 2005) commenting on Philip Roth's remarkable late-age productivity marveled at the fact that the author retained freedom from "performance-enhancing drugs." The implication is that if Roth were not "juiced," like O'Neill or Capote, how could he have written some of his best novels after the age of 60?

It is often assumed that artists live in the romantic tradition. John Cheever said that self-destruction is expected of the writer (Goodwin, 1988, p. 184). Indeed, the list of creative individuals who are or were famous addicts is remarkably long. The history of this connection dates back at least to the nineteenth century, when opium and opium-based products were widely used and sometimes abused by writers and poets. Along with Balzac, Dumas, and Flaubert, Baudelaire belonged to an elite group of French artists called the Hashish Club, led by novelist, Pierre Jules Theophile. Although the club's members met on a monthly basis to study the drug's effect on creativity, little is known about what they actually discovered. What does remain are Baudelaire's poetic renderings of the effects of wine and hashish:

> What man has never known the profound joys of wine? Whoever has had a grief to appease, a memory to evoke, a sorrow to drown, a castle in Spain to build – all have at one time invoked the mysterious god who lies concealed in the fibers of the grapevine. How radiant are those wine-induced visions, brilliantly illuminated by the inner sun! How true and burning this second youth which man calls wine. But how dangerous, too, are its fierce pleasures and debilitating enchantments.
>
> (Baudelaire, 1859/1996, p. 5)

For Baudelaire, intoxication clearly entailed a corporeal sublime state in which "we flutter towards infinity," with drunkenness leading to the "hypersublime."

In England, some Romantic poets matched the French in their use of opiates to foster creative inspiration. Shelley, Coleridge, Keats, and Byron used opium. John De Quincy's descriptions of opium's ability to enhance and even induce dream states in *Confessions of an English Opium-Eater* (1821/1950) are perhaps the most frequently cited in literature after those of Baudelaire. "The opium-eater," writes De Quincy, "feels that the diviner part of his nature is paramount; that is, the moral affections are in a state of cloudless serenity, and overall is the great light of the majestic intellect" (p. 37).

In the early twentieth century many American writers took to the bottle. These alcoholic writers included such luminaries as Edgar Allen Poe,

Theodore Dreiser, Hart Crane, Eugene O'Neill, Edna St. Vincent Millay, Dorothy Parker, Carson McCullers, F. Scott Fitzgerald, Dashiell Hammett, Wallace Stevens, E. E. Cummings, Theodore Roethke, Edmund Wilson, James Thurber, Jack London, Tennessee Williams, Truman Capote, Jack Kerouac, O. Henry, John Cheever, Conrad Aiken, Stephen Crane, William Saroyan, Irwin Shaw, Delmore Schwartz, Robert Lowell, Jean Stafford, James Agee, and Raymond Chandler. Nobel Prize-winning American writers who were alcoholics account for 70 percent of the American winners. Sinclair Lewis, William Faulkner, Ernest Hemingway, and John Steinbeck are among this elite cadre (Goodwin, 1988). In *Alcohol and the Writer*, Donald Goodwin (1988) claimed that alcoholism among writers reached epidemic proportions in America during the first half of the last century.

Why only the first half? Speculation tempts the reply that drugs trumped alcohol in the latter half of the century. In "The Rhetoric of Drugs," Jacques Derrida (2003) moved beyond the definition of addiction as the disease of modernity; he claimed that the birth of "narcotic modernity" is itself a cultural formation shaped by drugs. In the second half of the century, both jazz and rock musicians became tied to drug addiction. Reggae music, too, became associated with Bob Marley, Rastafarianism – and marijuana. Louis Armstrong was reputed to have smoked three huge joints every day of his life. Ray Charles is alleged to have written his best music during his 40-year heroin habit. Despite the notable accomplishments of drug-addicted artists, terrible casualties from drug overdoses unavoidably come to mind: Jimi Hendrix, Jim Morrison, Janis Joplin, Judy Garland, Billie Holiday, Elvis Presley, and Kurt Cobain all died before their time due to drug addiction. Jazz great, Charlie Parker, was said to have looked 30 years older than his age when he died from his well-known heroin habit.

Clearly, alcohol and drug addiction is not limited to writers and musicians. Many creative individuals in the entertainment industry, among them comedians and actors, have also succumbed to the allure of alcohol and other drugs. W. C. Fields, Buster Keaton, Bing Crosby, John Barrymore, Humphrey Bogart, Spencer Tracy, Ava Gardner, Marilyn Monroe, Elizabeth Taylor, John Belushi, and Robert Downey, Jr. are a few names that spring to mind. Beat generation writers, including Aldous Huxley, Allen Ginsberg, William Burroughs, and Henri Michaux experimented with LSD and mescaline. Elaine de Kooning (artist and wife of Willem de Kooning) reported that in 1950 "booze flooded the New York art scene" and "the whole art world became alcoholic" (Schildkraut, Hirshfeld, & Murphy, 1994, p. 485).

Unsurprisingly, for some, writing has become synonymous with alcoholism and music with narcotics addiction – the chemical omnipotently playing the role of both muse and demon. How is it that the relationship between artists and substance abuse is now taken as a given? Is such a tie justified or merely part of the popular myth of the unstable artist? And, if there is a strong bond between creativity and addiction, is the creative process helped or hindered by drugs? What meager literature exists on this rich subject consists of a few empirical studies, many of them from abroad.

The artist's pursuit of altered states

> In Xanadu did Kubla Khan
> A stately pleasure dome decree:
> Where Alph, the sacred river, ran
> Through caverns measureless to man
> Down to the sunless sea.
>   Samuel Coleridge

Like Coleridge, the archetypal Romantic poet and addict, who claimed to have written these opening lines to his famous poem, "Kubla Khan" (1899, p. 35), upon waking from an opium-induced dream state, other artists often sense that they are at the mercy of forces beyond their control. Jung (1952) addressed this phenomenon when he wrote about the artist as visionary, a passive instrument of his work, which has an agency and energy of its own. *The Strange Case of Dr. Jekyll and Mr. Hyde* (1886), similarly inspired by drug-induced dreams, apparently spilled from the pen of Robert Louis Stevenson during his six-day cocaine marathon. The author's proper and conscientious Edwardian physician, Dr. Jekyll, transmogrifying into the demonic Mr. Hyde, perfectly illustrates the capacity of substances to induce altered and uninhibited states of consciousness as well as overwhelm and even destroy the user.

Considering the question of why many artists rely on drugs, F. Scott Fitzgerald declared that creative vitality demands stimulation (Goodwin, 1988, p.187). Getting started is often deemed the most challenging aspect of creative work. E. B. White said he always treated himself to a dry martini in order to muster the courage to start writing. Indeed, many creative geniuses are convinced that the disinhibiting effect of alcohol provides them with the power to break through their blocks and fears.

Artists also use substances to perceive life through a new, fresher, or deeper lens, one difficult to come by naturally. Hallucinogens, or psychedelic drugs, allow the user to explore strange inner and outer worlds and their associated possibilities. The word "psychedelic" literally means to make the soul visible. Anaïs Nin expressed the novel perceptivity that LSD bestowed upon her, saying, "I could see a new world with my middle eye, a world I had missed before. I caught images behind images, the walls behind the sky, the sky behind the infinite" (Plant, 1999, p. 195). In *Alternating Current*, Octavio Paz wrote of the heightened emotional responsiveness and susceptibility inspired by drugs, saying that drugs "make the world a vast poem shaped by rhymes and rhythms" (Plant, 1999, p. 59). In the words of Stephen King, "The main effect of the grain or the grape on the creative personality is that it provides the necessary sense of newness and freshness, without which creative writing does not occur" (Goodwin, 1988, p. 187). Ten Berge (1999) employs the term "gaucherie" to describe the disinhibition frequently sought by creative artists. For example, some right-handed artists might deliberately work with their left hands. Some artists turn to substances to have their senses reinvigorated. John Cheever, who struggled with alcoholism, lamented that getting old dulls the senses. Some artists try to recapture a youthful – that is, wondrous, immediate, and full of possibility – way of encountering the world. When artists like Cheever experience the loss of this faculty, they may turn to substances in order to revive earlier states of knowing and feeling.

In 1859 Baudelaire wrote *Artificial Paradises*, a monograph that traced the transformations in thoughts and sensations that arose from smoking cannabis. He mentioned both euphoric and dysphoric reactions and elaborated on drug-induced *synesthesia*, a conflation of the senses (e.g. he described the sound of color and the color of sound) (Baudelaire, 1996/1859). In *Les Fleurs du Mal* (Flowers of Evil), he delineated the deleterious effects of hashish (1982). Anaïs Nin conveyed the hyperanesthetic and the synesthetic responses she had to LSD:

> The music vibrated through my body as if I were one of the instruments and I felt myself becoming a full percussion orchestra, becoming green, blue, orange. The waves of the sounds ran through my hair like a caress ... I was a cascade of red-blue rainfall, a rainbow, I was small, light, mobile.
>
> (Plant, 1999, p. 128)

The artist's omnipotent pursuit of altered states can be understood partially in terms of regressive phenomena – regression in a creative and non-pathological sense, with the goal of resurrecting early body states and object relations and inducing unconventional and unexpected modes of cognition. But now these earlier self-states and cognitive shifts arise within the frame of an induced alteration of consciousness that carries the intent to create. The regression is brought on and exists in symbiosis with the desire to fashion art. There is risk and danger in doing this, associated in particular with the dark side of addiction.

Ernst Kris (1952) saw the creative process as involving the phases of inspiration and elaboration. The *inspiration* state engulfs the artist in a rapturous feeling, which enables visionary insight and creates new constellations of meaning. In this state, even ontic and epistemological barriers are sometimes magically transcended. These altered states of consciousness return the artist to visceral possibilities and ways of thinking present in early life. Yet such states can exist once the world is known from a mature perspective, possibly only after one experiences the world as unpredictable and potentially disappointing. Furthermore, artists, like mystics, may be receptive to something not reducible to theory, a mystery neither inside nor outside, that cannot be objectified. In some Eastern philosophical traditions, for instance, drug usage is seen as allowing an omnipotent taste of the beyond, a kind of storming the temple of the All necessitated by the desire for transcendence (Feuerstein, 2001). Tribal people used drugs to enter into a state of spiritual ecstasy. Soma (an intoxicating juice) was drunk by the Vedic seers to write the sacred poems of the Rg Veda (de Nicholas, 1998; Feuerstein, 2001).

Kris's *elaboration* phase shapes the givens of the first phase. In this second phase, the raw product of the regression or altered state of mind is transformed into a recognizable and communicable form. It is at this point the private gift of the muse is transformed into a public offering. One writer described (to Knafo) it like this: "I write my first rough drafts while high on pot. The next day I read what I wrote and find mostly garbage, but also a few beautiful gems among the banana peels. I take those precious jewels, those resonant revelations, and then I connect them in a coherent way." Illustrating the two phases of creativity is a recurring motif on Grecian urns depicting Apollo, god of form and reason, holding the hand of Dionysius, god of intoxication, ecstasy, and intuition.

The sparse research that has been conducted on the effects chemicals (mostly alcohol) have on the creative process suggests that they may facilitate Kris's inspiration phase because they help to reduce blocks and censors, lessen inhibition, and induce relaxation after sustained effort (Koski-Jännes, 1985; Norlander, 1999). The saying "in vino veritas" reflects the longstanding belief that alcohol can be used to establish contact with deeper levels of the psyche (Ten Berge, 1999). On the other hand, alcohol appears more likely to hinder the second, elaboration, phase of the creative process because it relaxes the artist's focus and concentration, as well as reflective and critical faculties, all essential for the problem-solving and reality-testing facets of creativity. It has been found, for instance, that alcohol contributed to a weakening of secondary process thinking (Kalin, McClelland & Kahn, 1965; Gustafson & Källmén, 1989a, 1989b), damaging those skills responsible for the concrete, physical formation of an art product and its communication with the outside world. Hajcak's (1976) findings that alcohol enhanced originality but lowered creative problem-solving abilities further support the uneven effects alcohol has on the creative process. Norlander (1999) summed up the studies on alcohol and phases of the creative process as follows: "A moderate intake of alcohol obstructs those phases of creativity that are mainly based on the secondary process (preparation, certain phases of illumination, verification), but facilitates those phases mainly based on the primary process (incubation, certain parts of illumination, restitution)" (p. 40). For instance, Storr (1976) claimed that marijuana inspired captivating melodies from his unconscious, yet lamented being unable to transcribe such melodies onto paper.

Using drugs or alcohol can also help some artists deal with specific anxieties that are aroused by the creative process itself. As one artist patient once told Dr. Knafo, "Art is a put up or shut up proposition. You jump off a cliff in the dark and pray your parachute opens." The risk of failure is great, and the stakes are very high because the intensity of serious creation, within and outside of art, requires one to be totally engaged and fully committed. Failure can bring deep despair. Furthermore, accessing unconscious material can be frightening and so deeply upsetting that it threatens ego integrity and the project itself. Knafo's artist patient mentioned above also said, "I love to roam the cosmic junkyard looking for new stuff, but it gets really dark out there, and the place is guarded by a pack of vicious hounds." Anxieties generated from the creative process may become crippling, and some artists use substances to bring them down to a level that permits the continuation of creative work.

The role of artistic sensitivity

The sensitivity of the artist is nearly a cliché. When she wrote about the childhood of artists, Phyllis Greenacre (1957/1971) emphasized their enhanced sensitivity to and perceptivity of their surroundings. Although the exquisitely attuned temperament may power creativity, it can also foster unbearable vulnerability, self-consciousness, sorrow, and a sense of meaninglessness (Jamison, 1993). Poet, playwright, drug addict, and quintessential madman of the modern avant-garde, Antonin Artaud recounted the excruciating quality of such an existence in *Lettres a Genica Athasiou*: "State of nerves, states of mind, state of the world. There are moments when the universe seems to resemble most closely a scalp quivering with electric jolts" (quoted in Weiss, 2003, p. 161). Expanding on Artaud's poignant description, editor William McIlwain said that "a writer perhaps can't stand all the things he sees clearly and … must take the white glare out of the clarity" (Goodwin, 1988, p. 169). Some artists remove the "white glare" by seeking substances that dull the pain of extreme sensitivity. Canadian author Malcolm Lowry seemed to agree with McIlwain when he professed that he lacked the usual filters. In fact, Lowry felt that he'd been born without a skin, alleging his drinking prevented a nervous breakdown (Goodwin, 1988, p. 169). Like Lowry, Robert Lowell wrote of "seeing too much and feeling it with one skin layer missing" (Jamison, 1993, p. 117).

Artaud, Lowry, Lowell, and many other creative individuals are painfully sensitive and attend too minutely to their environment and suffer sensory overload as a result. Invaded by a constant stream of disruptive and irritating stimuli, they use substances to moderate or extinguish the "afferent" side of their talent, which emancipates them from sensorial tyranny and haunting memories. Furthermore, the insecurity inherent in living a creative life derives from a number of sources, not the least of which is the constant confrontation with one's own limitations in previously untested arenas, only to have those limits scrutinized and evaluated on a constant basis. Such insecurity in artists' lives combines with an already sensitive nature. Jazz musician Stan Kenton (1960) maintained that "it's hard for the average person who isn't creative to know what a terrible insecurity exists within someone who dared to be different, and you have to dare to be different if you're going to create anything fresh" (p. 38).

Andy, a novelist, betrayed his exquisite sensitivity during a session when he told Dr. Knafo:

> One of the earliest memories I have is crying because the yolk of my egg ran out, while there was still plenty of white left. After that I only wanted eggs scrambled. I know it sounds silly, but it wasn't the yoke running out in itself that set me off. It was the first time I realized that things did run out. Stuff breaks. People get old. Everything changes. Life is finite. That's why I cried, and even though at the time I didn't clearly realize such formulations, I sensed at a deep level that the very fabric of life is made up of change and depletion.

Sensitivity, shyness, insecurity, and isolation are bound to coexist in the lives of many, if not most, creative individuals. Creativity is a solitary occupation; time spent alone is needed to generate and implement ideas. Such requisite isolation offers an escape from the stress of social situations, but it also produces loneliness and requires the creative person to labor for extended periods of time with little or no emotional support from others. Substances like alcohol are known to provide courage for those who lack it and companionship for those who seek it. Writers are loners and alcohol is a loner's disease, says Goodwin (1988, p. 180). Writing and drugs are two forms of companionship. "It's my life, it's my wife," sang Lou Reed of his heroin; William Burroughs referred to his "old friend Opium Jones" (Odier, 1970, p. 151). Director (2002) perceptively claimed that a relational impasse underlies most compulsive substance abuse.

Sensitivity involves a greater capacity for feeling, emotional reactions, and tolerance of extreme affective states. Ironically, it is the artists' inordinate sensitivity that provides the link between creativity and mood disorder. In 1921, Emil Kraeplin delineated the positive aspects of manic-depressive illness by mentioning its connection to creativity:

> The volitional excitement which accompanies the disease may under certain circumstances set free powers which otherwise are constrained by all kinds of inhibition. Artistic activity namely may, by the untroubled surrender to momentary fancies or moods, and especially poetical activity by the facilitation of linguistic expression, experience a certain furtherance.
>
> (p. 17)

The connection between mood disorder and creativity is one that has been underscored in several studies. For example, Richards and her colleagues (1988) observed that a genetic predisposition to manic-depressive illness accompanied a parallel predisposition to creativity. They found significantly higher scores on creativity measures among manic-depressives and cyclothymics, as well as their first-degree relatives, than in controls. Jamison (1989) similarly found that 38 percent of the outstanding British writers and artists she studied had been treated for affective illness. In 1993, she cited an impressive list – which includes the likes of Lord Byron, Robert Schumann, Herman Melville, Ernest Hemmingway, Virginia Woolf, Alfred Tennyson, Vincent van Gogh, F. Scott Fitzgerald, and Robert Lowell – to make a convincing argument for the "compelling association, not to say actual overlap, between two temperaments – the artistic and the manic-depressive – and their relationships to the rhythms and cycles, or temperament, of the natural world" (p. 5). She referred to the episodic or cyclic nature observable in both creativity and bipolar illness.

In addition to demonstrating how the temperaments of artists and individuals with bipolar disorder are equally characterized by sensitivity and imagination, Jamison explained how both manic and depressive aspects of the illness are capable of stimulating creativity. Perhaps the manic episode more obviously resembles creative processes in its frenzied excitement, *visionary grandiosity*, and generation of ideas and connections. The fluency, fluidity, and frequency of thoughts and associations, the intensity of emotional experience and expression, and the sharp focus and power of concentration are present in both hypomanic and creative states. In fact, one criterion for diagnosing mania involves original thinking, heightened sensitivity, and increased productivity (American Psychiatric Association, 2013). Neurologist Robert DeLong (1990) found that children who display early signs of bipolar illness show significantly more imagination than most children. Of course, shorter art forms, like poetry or painting, are more easily created in a period of hypomania than others (e.g. longer writing projects) that require sustained effort over a number of months (Andreason & Glick, 1988). Fitzgerald once apologized to his editor for his excessive drinking while writing *Tender Is the Night*, explaining that "a short story can be written on a bottle, but for a novel you need the mental speed that enables you to keep the whole pattern in your head" (Goodwin, 1988, p. 43).

Depression, too, encourages creativity in its sensitivity and compassion for the human condition as well as in its inward gazing and rumination. In their book, *Saturn and Melancholy* (1964), Klibansky, Panofsky, and Saxl demonstrated how poetic melancholy is essentially an enhanced self-awareness. By cooling the ardor of mania, depression allows the slower pace necessary for the shaping and production of art, Kris's elaboration phase.

Not surprisingly, substance abuse plays a role in the intimate link between mood disorder and creativity. Andreason (1987) conducted a 15-year study of creative writers from the Iowa Writer's Workshop and compared them with a control group of non-writers matched for age, sex, education, and intelligence. The group of writers were more often depressed (37%), more often manic

(43%), and more often alcoholic (30%) compared with 7 percent in the comparison group of non-writers. Overall, she found that 80 percent of the writer study sample met criteria for major affective disorder. Ludwig (1994) noted that Andreason's sample consisted primarily of male subjects and therefore tried to determine whether similar trends exist in a sample of women writers. He matched 59 women writers with a comparable sample of 59 non-writers and found that 56 percent were depressed (vs. 14% controls), 19 percent manic (vs. 3% controls), and 17 percent drug addicts (vs. 5% controls).

A most useful way to comprehend the significant relationships that exist among alcoholism, drugs, mood disorder, and writing is to consider how writers (and other artists) may use and abuse alcohol (as well as additional substances) to regulate their feelings and sensibilities. Whereas Andreason's study observed that writers are at the very minimum 30 percent more inclined to have mood disorders and to be alcoholics than her non-writer sample, it has also been found that at least 30 percent of addicts suffer from serious affective disorders (Krystal, 1995). Schildkraut, Hirshfeld, and Murphy (1994), in their study of New York Abstract Expressionist artists, found that over 50 percent of the artists they studied had some form of psychopathology, predominantly mood disorders and preoccupation with death, often compounded by alcohol or drug abuse. Once again, 30 percent had substance-abuse histories.

Obviously, the studies mentioned above indicate a strong relationship between mood disorder and substance abuse but fail to clarify which comes first or how one contributes to the other. Krystal (1982, 1995) argued most convincingly that addicts employ substances to recognize and tolerate their emotional states. Here the condition is seen to precede the substance abuse. Khantzian (1995, 1999), too, proposed that addicts self-medicate and find a "drug of choice," or a combination of substances, to regulate difficult affect states. Therefore, what we observe is the transformative effect of drugs in their capacity to create a comfort zone for the artist who uses them. It is not merely about creating art; it is often about creating some ease in order to live. However, the very act of self-medication can eventually unleash the destructive and disruptive effects of addiction. Burroughs wrote that hashish "makes a bad situation worse. Depression becomes despair, anxiety panic" (quoted in Plant, 1999, p. 36).

The sensitivity attributed to the artistic temperament is regrettably the same sensitivity that may open doors to depression and to an intimacy with life's darker forces. Melancholia, or depression, involves a painful sensitivity, an unwavering vision that considers reality, morbidity, and death with less denial and sanitization than a "normal" frame of mind. Segal (1991) linked depression, with its accent on mourning, to the capacity for symbolization. Interestingly, the word "symbol" derives from the Greek *symbolen*, which means to reunite. Symbolization, then, can be thought of as the ability to ponder and realize what is absent. Through symbolization, we magically repair and reunite with whom and what has been lost to us. The depressive perspective, by definition, is one that embraces a particular and darker view of the human condition and does not shy away from experiencing guilt, loss, and the inevitability and finality of death. Such terror-driven experiences can act as a bittersweet muse to the creative process, yet they can also be felt as unbearable and lead to addiction. Baudelaire wrote:

> One must always be intoxicated. That's the main thing; it's the only issue. In order to feel the horrible burden of Time which breaks your shoulders and bows you to earth, you must become intoxicated without respite.
>
> (1974, p. 5)

Ultimately, one can say that it is the burden of mortality which is most deeply felt, though perhaps also denied, by one possessing the sensitivity of an artist.

Omnipotent fantasies provide a sense of comfort and protection from the terror of mortality. Moreover, through these fantasies transformations of self can take place when creative efforts draw from the same pool that creates the magic of childhood. Fantasies underlying creativity can serve to recreate relationships with others or to fill the void left by those who went missing or never showed up. Omnipotent fantasies can also nurture growth and foster the development of a strong sense of self. Rather than submitting to the harsh circumstances of reality, magical illusions can provide a person with a fantastical sense of control. These fantasies provide artists with the power to construct the world in ways that match the world they need.

Part II

Messages in a bottle: Literary and clinical applications

Chapter 4

The black art of Anne Sexton

> You write for an audience (I think of myself as writing for one person, that one perfect reader who understands and loves). If the audiences were this one person multiplied by a hundred or a thousand, everything would be okeydokey.
>
> Anne Sexton (1973/1985e, p. 33)

For Anne Sexton, poetry and addiction went hand-in-hand – partners in crime facilitating her most exhilarating highs and debilitating lows. This was no secret to her family, friends, colleagues, and fans. When she toured the country for readings, she traveled with a thermos of martinis. She was famous for standing barefoot at the podium with a drink in one hand and a cigarette in the other (Middlebrook, 1991). Her psychiatrist nurtured her creativity, and Sexton began to express her most intimate personal experiences on paper, then became immensely popular for speaking the unspeakable in public forums (Middlebrook, 1991). Her autobiographical confessions radically transformed poetry and brought out others who had lived their entire lives in hiding – alone with their shame of mental illness, fraught sexuality, addictions, relationship difficulties, and suicidal thoughts. It was not exactly common in the 1960s for women to discuss scandalous love affairs, bisexuality, abortion, and the hypocrisy of middle-class suburbia – particularly not in front of large crowds of people (Middlebrook, 1991). Nonetheless, even those who were not necessarily fans of poetry found themselves drawn to the raw human emotion expressed in Sexton's writing. The poet Sylvia Plath wrote in the confessional mode in the same era, but Anne Sexton, following Plath's path, took the genre even further, as she plumbed the depths of her anguish and existential despair.

The self-exposure and self-revelation Sexton achieved through her confessional poetry became addictive to her (Hughes, 1991). She fantasized that, through her poems, she could not only save herself, but also powerfully affect others because "that's what a poem should do – move people to action" (Sexton, 1974/1985a, p. 89). Sexton strove to transform the world through the magical ability of stringing together the perfect sequence of words. And in many ways, she did see her omnipotent fantasies materialize in the external world. She became known for changing the landscape of conventional poetry, and she helped to turn traditional gender roles on their head. By the end of her life, she had received countless awards and honors, including the Pulitzer Prize, the Levinson Prize for Poetry, several nominations for the National Book Award, and a number of highly prestigious fellowships for her writing. Sexton believed that her psychoanalytic treatment offered her access to the unconscious part of her mind – both beautiful and repulsive – from which rich poetic truths flowed. But, like many artists whose creativity leaves an indelible footprint on the cultural terrain, the workshop in Sexton's mind was also a place of tremendous suffering.

Despite the enormous success, praise, and adulation Sexton received from fans and critics alike, her internal detractors grew more powerful in her final years. Whereas her attunement to tragedy allowed her to capture the absurdities of human struggles with striking poignancy, this same sensitivity precipitated her self-destruction. Sexton proclaimed that, in addition to having developed a taste for alcohol and drugs, she was also attracted to death, declaring that "suicide is addicting too" (Middlebrook, 1991, p. 200). Sexton's creativity was fueled in part by the disinhibiting properties of alcohol and prescription pills, but these magical potions also exacerbated her emotional problems and resulted in the addiction that finally consumed her. From an early age, both Sexton's poetry and substance abuse served as potent magic wands with which she sought to transform the frightening "truths" of her inner and outer realities. Sexton's creativity burned bright across the span of her life in the flames of omnipotence forged in the utter helplessness she experienced in her earliest relationships. Those flames also fueled her addictions and mood disorder, as well as other tendencies to self-sabotage – for instance, in interpersonal relationships. This chapter examines the omnipotent fantasies in Sexton's life and those which drove many of her poems.

Magical words: omnipotence and creativity

In a letter addressed to one of her first writing mentors, Sexton announced, "poetry has saved my life" (Sexton & Ames, 1977, p. 39). This rather succinct statement speaks volumes about the omnipotent value Sexton placed on her poetry – both as a protective shield and a mighty weapon. As she once put it, "Words do not tell the truth … they control it; they are ritual and magic" (Colburn, 1988, p. 225). For Sexton, a well-crafted poem acted for both the writer and reader as a portal to the unconscious truths essential to great poetry:

> You need courage to overcome the little inherent deceits in yourself and stamina to bring the truth alive in a poem … In some ways, as you see me now, I am a lie. The crystal truth is in my poetry.
>
> (Sexton, 1968/1985b, p. 115)

Sexton's poetry gave her the courage to endure the painful truths shadowing her since childhood. She believed that she had been "a girl who was meant to be a boy, the unwanted third daughter" (Sexton & Ames, 1977, p. 3). Born into a prosperous family, she grew up in a four-story house complete with servants' quarters. Her parents were young and preoccupied with status, and their parenting took second place to their social obligations and activities (Boler, 2004). Sexton's recollections highlight the shame, humiliation, and conflicting messages she received from her parents:

> Disgusted, mother put me
> on the potty. She was good at this.
> My father was fat on scotch.
> It leaked from every orifice.
> Oh the enemas of childhood,
> reeking of outhouses and shame!
> Yet you rock me in your arms
> and whisper my nickname.
> (Sexton, 1965/1999a,
> pp. 160–161)

Sexton described her initial interest in becoming a poet as an attempt to be lovable and to feel loved. Before she could read or write, she learned that writers topped the social hierarchy (Middlebrook, 1991). While writing little more than letters, both her mother and grandfather were designated as the "writers" of the family (Middlebrook, 1991). As a child, Sexton felt that she had little to offer her parents as a means of gaining their love. She fantasized that if she took up the idealized family trade, perhaps they would finally shower her with the love she craved; they would recognize her as a *real* person, their daughter, someone they cherished and appreciated (Sexton & Ames, 1977). She once stated how winning the love of her fans became symbolic of her desperate need to be loved and admired, particularly by her mother (Sexton, 1976/1999d, p. 529).

During adolescence and into early adulthood, Sexton clung to the hope that poetry was the key to her mother's heart (Sexton & Ames, 1977). Her first poems were written at age 17 in an effort to make sense of a romantic relationship that ended in heartbreak (Middlebrook, 1991). For instance, in "Killing the Love," she wrote: "I am the love killer, / I am murdering the music we thought so special, / that blazed between us, over and over" (Sexton, 1976/ 1999d, p. 529). By transcribing her feelings into words, Sexton believed she could keep them alive while assuming mastery over those feelings. She once said, "I have this great need somehow to keep that time of my life, that feeling. I want to imprison it in a poem, to keep it" (Sexton, 1966/1985d, p. 74).

Sexton quickly learned that gaining the acceptance of her parents would not be easy nor follow the script of her fantasies. Mary Gray Sexton was fiercely competitive with her daughter. She accused her of plagiarism when her school yearbook published one of Sexton's earliest poems, arguing that it was "too good" to be her own. She even sent her daughter's poem to an expert in the hopes of proving the allegation. Sexton later attributed Mary Gray's hurtful gesture to a need that her mother keep "top billing" in the family as "writer." Although the college professor who judged the yearbook poem's authenticity ruled that not only was the work most likely original but it also showed great promise, Sexton said she was too hurt and discouraged to write another poem for the next ten years (Middlebrook, 1991).

Reviving creativity in psychoanalysis

Over a decade later, after entering psychoanalysis following her first suicide attempt and hospitalization, Sexton's creativity was revived. Her treatment with Dr. Orne marked the beginning of Sexton's discovery of purpose: the raw expression of emotion. Although she initially proposed to him that her only talent might best fit a career as a prostitute, Dr. Orne's assessment was that his patient had vast creative potential. Early into the treatment, he encouraged Sexton to write about her suffering and personal experiences, suggesting that her poetry could help others struggling with similar conditions to feel less alone (Skorczewski, 2012). Hearing this, Sexton felt she was being treated as a "capable person" for the first time (Middlebrook, 1991, p. 42) and hoped her personal poems could "become the central theme to someone else's private life" (Sexton, 1968/1985c, p. 50).

When Sexton began sharing her poetry with Dr. Orne, he consistently praised her, in stark contrast to the way her mother had responded to her writing. That sort of encouragement was exactly what she needed, and her writing began to flourish. She produced at least 60 new poems over the course of her first year in treatment. Sexton recalled, "I kept writing and writing and giving them all to him ... I kept writing because he was approving" (as cited in Middlebrook, 1991, p. 42). She reported that following one suicide attempt, Dr. Orne told her, "You can't kill yourself, you have something to give. Why, if people read your poems (they were all about how sick I was) they would think, 'There's somebody else like me!' They wouldn't feel alone" (pp. 42–43). This moment was a profound turning point in Sexton's life. "I had found something to *do* with my life," she said (p. 43).

When Sexton began attending writing workshops and meeting fellow writers, she recalled feeling at home for the first time. "The most important aspect of the class was that I felt I belonged somewhere ... I felt, 'These are my people.' ... I found I belonged to the poets, that I was *real* there ..." (as cited in Middlebrook, 1991, p. 50). At her psychiatrist's urgings, Sexton began submitting her poetry for publication. When she first received the news that her work had been accepted, she met with a response from her father that was hurtful and troublesome. Although her father seemed proud enough to brag to his business colleagues about his daughter's publications, he made certain that Sexton never forgot her place beneath her mother in the ranking of most valuable family writers. Sexton's father resolutely declared: "None of you girls are as brilliant as your mother. You are creative but she is brilliant" (p. 20).

As heartbreaking as this response might have been for Sexton, there was no quelling the creative spark that had been ignited in her analysis. Perhaps her father's efforts to devalue her first glimpse of success added fuel to the fire, especially in light of her increasing defiance and castigation of the patriarchy emerging in her poems. Partly as a consequence of postwar America's idealization of woman as housewife, Sexton quickly found that the familial conflicts she battled were common in her social circle of writers. Writing became a powerful tool for women to work against the constrictions of social conventions, and Sexton and her circle wrote literature supporting the feminist cause. Sexton herself made a career of violating the era's social taboos: "One can't build little white picket fences to keep the nightmares out" (Sexton, 1974/1985a, p. 84).

Omnipotent fantasies of transforming the social scene, overthrowing the current value system, and changing the world drove her fierce creative energies. And while perhaps laden with narcissistic illusions, Sexton's fantasies received confirmation in the "real" world. In her hopes of someday being remembered among the greats, she said,

> Kafka, Dostoevsky are great because of the effect of their work. It's still going on; they are dead but it's still going on with the same impact as if they were alive. Their lives were messes but it doesn't make any difference – what they *did* was more important than a good life.
> (Sexton, as cited in Middlebrook, 1991, p. 165)

Sexton associated her efforts to write with strivings to maintain ties to her mother, once stating in a letter addressed to Mary Gray, "I love you. I don't write for you, but know that one of the reasons I do write is that you are my mother" (Sexton & Ames, 1977, p. 30). When Mary Gray was diagnosed with breast cancer, Sexton's conflicted feelings became more intense: "Mother makes me sick but I love her ... Part of me would be free if she died. It would also be awful – I would dissolve" (Middlebrook, 1991, pp. 46–47). Ironically, following surgery to treat her cancer, Mary Gray offered Sexton her first message of encouragement: "You have something to give – a word – the word – a beautiful appreciation of what life – nature – and human relationship does" (p. 47).

Throughout her treatment in psychoanalysis, Sexton gained insight into the far-reaching effects of her conflicted feelings toward her mother – those of dependency and love, a desperate need for approval, simmering resentment, and bright rage. In her journal, Sexton declared, "The great theme we all share is that of becoming ourselves, of overcoming our father and mother, of assuming our identities somehow" (Sexton & Ames, 1977, p. 26). Eventually, Sexton came to accept the strength she acquired through identification with her mother. She told Dr. Orne, "[Mother's] father was a writer and she should have been a writer – I'm my mother, only I did it and she didn't" (Middlebrook, 1991, p. 49).

The best revenge

Sexton's rising star as a poet tantalized her parents; she achieved what they could not. They would finally realize that their daughter, whom they had dismissed, degraded, and outright rejected, had become the symbol of what they had most coveted.

Sexton often attributed her powerful attachment to her psychiatrist to her efforts to substitute his love for what her parents proved unable to give. Dr. Orne's affirmations filled the vast inner emptiness she experienced every day (Skorczewski, 2012, p. 4). Calling it "an accident of hope," Sexton began to see her poetry as both the product of and cure for her psychological suffering. In a number of sessions, she proposed that her poetry signaled progress in her treatment (Skorczewski, 2012, pp. 2–3). Dr. Orne audiotaped the therapy sessions with Sexton during the last three of the eight years he worked with her in order to help her remember what transpired in the sessions. These recordings, claimed Skorczewski (2012), "depict a very sick woman becoming well as she crafted poems, studied the art of poetry, and made connections with academics and writers" (p. xix).

Indeed, Sexton's unbridled drive to succeed as a poet was relentless. The inner strength that the praise of critics, fans, and admirers instilled in her seemed limitless at times. In the wake of her earliest literary achievements, Sexton displayed remarkable resilience to the narcissistic injuries a young writer typically faces. When her work was returned with a rejection slip, Sexton would almost immediately resubmit it elsewhere. During that time, it was typical for her to resubmit the same poem 12 or 15 times in the same year (Middlebrook, 1991).

Sexton's poems often articulated her fantasies of both creating life and taking it away through the command of her words. Her poems also expressed an all-powerful capacity to obliterate her suicidal urges with the masterful influence of her creativity (Skorczewski, 2012, p. 23). "Suicide is, after all, the opposite of the poem," she once declared (George, 1987, para. 6). Transforming her suicidal impulses into poetry provided Sexton with a sense of control over such potentially lethal affective states (Skorczewski, 2012). She often explained to Dr. Orne how her writing kept her suicidal urges at bay: "I'd rather be doing something productive than sitting around thinking about killing myself – or killing myself," she said. "I put some aggression into something constructive. Cheered me up" (Middlebrook, 1991, p. 52).

While the omnipotence at the source of Sexton's poetry had adaptive capability, her narcissistic illusions came with their own set of complications.

Outside the magic circle of poetry, she battled the threat of internally destructive forces. In her work with Dr. Orne, Sexton's insatiable need for affirmation as a writer became the focus of the treatment. Reluctant to validate Sexton's experience of poetry as her "only accomplishment," he said, "you keep wanting me to be more interested in your poems than in you" (Skorczewski, 2012, p. 6). Sexton was adamant about her poetic purpose, and said, during the late stages of her treatment, that having accomplished what she had set out to do in her writing, she was now prepared to die (Skorczewski, 2012).

Although poetry may have forestalled her death, the destructive forces of her depression and suicidal urges overshadowed the more adaptive features of her narcissistic illusions. Sexton's poetry gave her a great sense of control over her feelings and the events in her life, but so too did the promise of suicide. Outraged by the suicide of Sylvia Plath, she told Dr. Orne that she felt robbed by her fellow poet and friend's death. Sexton dreamed of someday immortalizing her legendary status as a poet by taking her own life, thereby affecting legions of loving and admiring fans. She expressed feeling envious and angry that Plath had done it first. Sexton may have conceived of suicide as a performance sacrifice to gain immortality, a kind of heroic death. In this omnipotent fantasy, life is replaced with a death that is greater than life, and Sexton kills herself to animate her legend. It could be, however, that she was weary and broken, and had few words left to cast her magic circle. Perhaps both motives were operating. Sexton often confessed that she had become "addicted to death," addicted to the impulse to destroy herself. By taking her own life, she could substantiate the grandiose image of herself as an all-powerful force able to control the pain she experienced and destroy the ugliness of the external world that she felt so vividly. She believed that, as a writer, she felt too much, and that alcohol and prescription drugs took the edge off those intolerable feelings.

A mother, but better

Like the narcissistic illusions powering her creative drive, Sexton's substance abuse was deeply embedded in fantasies tied to her relationships with her parents. As the owner of a wool manufacturing business booming in the war economy, Sexton's father Ralph Harvey had enough free time to drink the days away. When he no longer had to work as a traveling salesman, he sequestered himself in his room with a bottle of whiskey for company. Sexton described how he regularly emerged heavily intoxicated and "would suddenly just become very mean, as if he hated the world" (Middlebrook, 1991, p. 14). The verbal abuse she endured from her drunken father destroyed her trust in his love. When Sexton was going through puberty, her father once drunkenly stormed off from dinner in a fit of disgust, complaining that the sight of her acne had made him lose his appetite (Sexton & Ames, 1977, p. 12).

Sexton's mother's drinking habits were not as extreme as her husband's; however, Mary Gray's personality became frighteningly erratic when she drank. Sexton's sister Jane once described the contrasting temperaments of their parents in a letter, stating, "Daddy was either drunk or sober ... But you never knew, with Mother, when she was going to be horrible or nice. The minute you thought you knew where you were, she'd turn on you" (Middlebrook, 1991, p. 13). Sexton recalled that her mother would drink "any time she wanted" (p. 13), implying that Mary Gray had no control over her alcohol use. Sexton often requested that, like her mother, she be referred to as a "drunk" rather than an alcoholic (p. 13). Mary Gray did not like the stigma associated with the term "alcoholism," and neither did Sexton.

As much as Sexton identified with the excessiveness of her parents' drinking, she also despised it. The conscious, rational part of her mind knew that alcohol had made a significant contribution to the interpersonal devastation her family endured, but the unconscious part drove her forth in search of a bottle containing the panacea for her misery. By the time she was 15, Sexton felt as though her entire family was crumbling around her, recalling, "My father was drinking every minute, Nana was going crazy, my grandfather was crazy, Jane was having a baby" (Middlebrook, 1991, p. 16). In search of a welcomed retreat from her volatile home life, Sexton developed an active social life in high school and began a series of intimate relationships and an instant attachment to alcohol.

At age 20, although Sexton was already engaged to another man, she met, fell in love with, and married Alfred "Kayo" Sexton. But not much more than a year later, Sexton fell desperately in love with another man. When her mother insisted that she put an end to the affair and see a psychiatrist, Sexton overdosed on sleeping pills. Perhaps, in fantasy, the pills were a means to gaining a sense of control over a world that felt too much to bear. Sexton later described her suicidal behavior and alcohol use as a constructive effort: "It's not that I'm killing myself but that I'm controlling myself. Also when I drink. I'd really be a mess if I quit" (Boler, 2004, p. 113).

When Sexton's poetry began to receive widespread acclaim in the 1960s, the pressures of fame increased her addictive behavior. After being nominated for a National Book Award, she reached for the bottle as great demands were placed on her to give interviews and present her work across the country. Although the acclaim may have bolstered Sexton's sense of self-worth and identity, it also frightened her, which is why she drank during readings. It was Sexton's daughter Linda Gray who, at the age of eight, prepared her mother's martinis for her readings (Boler, 2004).

Linda Gray (Sexton & Ames, 1977) has said that as her mother's life was nearing its end, her addictions escalated, her personality grew more shrill and demanding, and her behavior more outrageous and erratic. In preparation for a series of readings in the South, Sexton wrote the organizers, "If Virginia is a 'dry' state [this letter is] to prepare you for my need of a semi-wet before dinner and a reading" (Boler, 2004, p. 114). She brought vials of vodka wherever she went, even when attending faculty meetings at Boston University, where she held a teaching position. It was during one of these meetings that Sexton was famously caught in the act of passing a small bottle of vodka to a colleague and fellow alcoholic (Middlebrook, 1991).

After she won the Pulitzer Prize in 1967, Sexton's substance abuse soared to new heights along with her reputation. She became addicted to barbiturates and other prescription drugs, continued to drink vodka before her poetry readings, and took pills afterwards. Sexton's creative potential eventually deteriorated as a result of alcohol and prescription medications. By the early 1970s, she drank from morning until night, and many critics and fans alike agreed that her addictions were ruining her ear, killing her skill for finding the subtle rhythm so essential to the spellbinding verse that had made her famous (Salvio, 2007). The war between the urge for self-destruction and personal growth was not going well.

In her early poetry, Sexton sometimes depicted alcohol as her muse, but as her disease progressed, this sentiment changed: "What kills the creative instinct – what blunts the ax? Liquor and other devices. Of course they blunt my pain, too ... Maybe I'll have to do without my crutches" (as cited in Middlebrook, 1991, p. 198). In the following excerpt from her biography, Middlebrook describes Sexton's double bind:

> Alcohol helped generate the curves of feeling on which her poetry lifted its wings, but it dropped her too, into depression, remorse, sleeplessness, paranoia – the normal host of furies that pursue alcoholics. More serious for her poetry, it deprived her of "the little critic" in her head that she had formerly summoned to the task of cut, cut, cut, expand, expand, expand, cut, cut, cut. She had the drunk's fluency but not the artist's cunning.
>
> (Middlebrook, 1991, pp. 379–380)

As the pressures to live up to extraordinary expectations increased, Sexton's fears of failing grew, creating even more need to impress her admirers, which plunged her deeper into her addiction in a desperate effort to maintain the illusion of omnipotent control. Sexton admitted that she was "worried about failure. Artists always are" (as cited in Middlebrook, 1991, p. 198). Intense fear of failure is indeed common among artists and can become sharpest immediately following success. The prospect of never topping themselves again, that they have peaked for good, that their subsequent work will always pale in comparison, are often the cause for a sudden, rampant increase in self-destructive behaviors.

Sexton knew what she was doing to herself, even as she hid from it. Through years of treatment, she gained insight into the relationship between her personality and her addictions; addictions and her parents; and her drive to live and desire to die. Reflecting on the insights she gleaned from writing poetry, Sexton said, "[My] poetry is more advanced, in terms of my unconscious, than I am. Poetry, after all, milks the unconscious. The unconscious is there to feed it little images, little symbols, the answers, the insights I know not of" (Sexton, 1974/1985a, p. 85). In a session with Dr. Orne, she shared a chilling insight:

> My mother drank two drinks every noon and three drinks every night come hell or high water ... My father would drink on the sly, by the case ... I still have the glasses they had in the twenties – I thought, my God, this is justice: my parents drank themselves into the grave and now I'm drinking out of the same glasses!
>
> (cited in Middlebrook, 1991, p. 13)

Yet insight never quite ended Sexton's dance with dangerous chemicals. The person revealed in such insight – herself – became the person she wished to avoid, as she plunged herself into extremes of work and inebriation. In one therapy session, Sexton explained to Dr. Orne that her numerous overdoses on pills had never been "real" suicide attempts but "substitutes":

> It's the same symbolic act, but there's a difference between taking something that will kill you and something that will kill you momentarily. The "kill me" pills are very special ... I stole them from my parents ... I raided the poisons ... If I didn't have Deprol and Nodular as substitutes I'm sure I'd be dead by now – get rid of that girl out in the suburbs!
>
> (Middlebrook, 1991, p. 165)

Milking the unconscious

For Sexton, poetry was a confessional art: one that promoted healing in both author and reader. Whereas Sexton often felt no control over the circumstances of her life and the emotional wounds she suffered, her words offered magic promises about possessing the capacity to transform herself and the world around her.

Sexton grappled with many complex personal problems that she revealed in letters, interviews, the tapes of her psychoanalysis with Dr. Orne, and other sources of self-expression. Perhaps even more spellbinding than the self-portraits she painted in her conscious communications with others are the complex and deeply personal themes that run through her poetry. Her poems opened portals into hermetically sealed-off emotional experiences – many concealed from both herself and others. In particular, a fierce conflict often emerged over her need to break through the stifling limitations of her humanity versus the insidious pull to bury herself and literally put an end to her existence. For instance, in her poem "Civil War," Sexton's will to overcome the urge to destroy herself and resilience are highlighted in the ways in which she separates parts of herself into two distinct modes of experience:

> I am torn in two
> but I will conquer myself.
> I will dig up the pride.
> I will take scissors
> and cut out the beggar.
> I will take a crowbar
> and pry out the broken pieces of God in me.
> Just like a jigsaw puzzle,
> I will put Him together again
> with the patience of a chess player.
> (Sexton, 1975/1999h, p. 418)

The split in self-states reflects the paradox of Sexton's omnipotent fantasies – "God in me" – especially those that led her to discover her life-promoting creative self. Her omnipotent fantasies clashed with her experience of herself as flawed, which often sent Sexton falling back into the grips of addictions and other forms of self-destruction.

In addition to its personal connotations, "Civil War" is exemplary of the prominence of Sexton's transcendent self at the time. She started out as a trailblazer who challenged traditional mid-century American values. The title "Civil War" foreshadows Sexton's influence over the burgeoning "civil war" of the Women's Rights Movement in the 1960s, wherein Sexton impacted American perceptions of traditional values regarding perceptions of female equality.

Like most counterculture movements, Sexton rapidly encountered the backlash of critics, even those close to her. For instance, she was urged by her writing mentor John Holmes to tone down what he deemed to be excessively intimate details of her personal life. In "For John, Who Begs Me Not to Enquire Further," Sexton reacted to Holmes's criticism, vehemently defending her raw self-exposure, and not always pretty, autobiographical style:

> Not that it was beautiful,
> but that, in the end, there was
> a certain sense of order there;
> something worth learning
> in that narrow diary of my mind,
> in the commonplaces of the asylum
> where the cracked mirror
> or my own selfish death
> outstared me.
> And if I tried

> to give you something else,
> something outside of myself,
> you would not know
> that the worst of anyone
> can be, finally,
> an accident of hope.
>   (Sexton, 1960/1999b, p. 34)

The above poem illustrates the growth-promoting aspects of Sexton's fantasies of limitlessness, tearing down the standards of traditional poetry and overall cultural etiquette in mid-century America. With the raw emotion, intimacy, and truths expressed in her poetry – no matter how distasteful or grotesque to some segments of the population – Sexton believed she could attain the contact she longed for. In "The Ambition Bird," she described fantasies that the power of her poetry would set her free – and perhaps keep her alive:

> The business of words keeps me awake.
> I would like a simple life
> yet all night I am laying
> poems away in a long box.
> It is my immortality box,
> my lay-away plan,
> my coffin.
> All night dark wings
> flopping in my heart.
> Each an ambition bird.
> The bird wants to be dropped
> from a high place like Tallahatchie Bridge.
> I must get a new bird
> and a new immortality box.
> There is folly enough inside this one.
>   (Sexton, 1972/1999g, pp. 299–300)

Sexton achieved a sense of mastery through illusions of omnipotent control; she created her own "immortality boxes." Her poetry transformed ugly emotions into beautiful words, the shame of isolation into coveted solitude, and passive protestations into frank and forthright communications. Most importantly, her poems kept her alive and promised immortality after her death. In both "For John, Who Begs Me Not to Enquire Further" and "The Ambition Bird," Sexton saw her words as the panaceas that would heal her suffering and the suffering of the world. Interestingly, these omnipotent fantasies about the potential power of her creativity were not just illusions.

Her omnipotent fantasies did not simply remain figments of Sexton's imagination. Readers embraced her poetry and were powerfully drawn to the

openness and authenticity in her work. Sexton also cleared a path for innovative self-expressions that developed in modern Reality TV, and the "tell-all"
memoirs of popular culture. And people will continue to appreciate and draw
meaning for their lives through her poems for years to come.

Nevertheless, in contrast to the two poems mentioned above as reflections
of Sexton's fantasies about words being all-powerful solutions, there are
others that exemplify a sense of worthlessness, shame, and deflated creativity.
When her reality betrayed her and her flaws were exposed, Sexton cried out in
agony, her wings scorched by the sun. Flying too high, or clinging rigidly to
narcissistic illusions about one's limitlessness, all too frequently plunged her
into the dark seas of debilitating depressions. This state is perhaps best captured in "The Silence":

> I am filling the room
> with the words from my pen ...
> Yet there is silence.
> Always silence ...
> The silence is death.
> It comes each day with its shock
> to sit on my shoulder ...
>   (Sexton, 1972/1999k,
>   pp. 318–319)

Sexton lamented the tortures she endured as a result of the heightened sensitivity required to create art. "A woman who writes feels too much," she wrote
in "The Black Art" (1965/1999a, pp. 88–89). Poetry represented the magic that
could float her to the highest heavens as well as the wrath that would inevitably
tear her down, striking the ground like a star falling from the sky. While
incredibly empowering, Sexton's writing career also at times felt to her like a
hopeless and futile endeavor (Middlebrook, 1991). In "Words," Sexton poignantly articulated the double-edged nature of her art, a sword that had the
potential to empower and protect as well as stab and wound.

> Be careful of words,
> even the miraculous ones.
> For the miraculous we do our best,
> sometimes they swarm like insects
>
> and leave not a sting but a kiss.
> They can be as good as fingers.
> They can be as trusty as the rock
> you stick your bottom on.
> But they can be both daisies and bruises.
> Yet I am in love with words.

They are doves falling out of the ceiling.
They are six holy oranges sitting in my lap.
They are the trees, the legs of summer,
and the sun, its passionate face.
Yet they often fail me.
I have so much I want to say,
so many stories, images, proverbs, etc.
But the words aren't good enough,
the wrong ones kiss me.
Sometimes I fly like an eagle
but with the wings of a wren.
But I try to take care
and be gentle to them.
Words and eggs must be handled with care.
Once broken they are impossible
things to repair.
                    (Sexton, 1975/1999m, pp. 463–464)

"Words" serves as a poignant reflection of Sexton's capacity to integrate her divided self, exhibited in her acceptance of the dual relationship she had forged with the power of her creativity. Sexton warned the reader – and herself – that such power can come at a terrible price. Not even the most perfect words can ultimately save anyone. Most important, words can never express everything we are feeling, but they are the best that we have.

An unnamable lust

While words may have been the best chance Sexton had to connect with herself and others, her creativity seemed to fail her more than she could tolerate. When discouraged by a creative block or feelings of deadness, Sexton took to alcohol and prescription pills, namely tranquilizers and stimulants. Interestingly, the extreme ups and downs of her omnipotence around creativity shaped and mirrored the patterns of her omnipotent fantasies around drugs – paralleling her fluctuating creative revelations in her use of "uppers" and "downers."

In "Frenzy," Sexton (1999c/1975) described the emotional whirlwind that would sweep her up in the euphoria of sudden inspiration and then leave her swirling in a dreadful downward spiral. She called the compulsion driving her creativity "the amphetamine of the soul," thus portraying her inspiration as an addictive force that could rival that of her substance use (p. 466). As the power of her creative energies waned, the bleak trajectory of her substance abuse was not far behind. In "The Addict," she wrote:

With capsules in my palms each night,
eight at a time from sweet pharmaceutical bottles

I make arrangements for a pint-sized journey.
I'm the queen of this condition.
I'm an expert on making the trip
and now they say I'm an addict.
Now they ask why.
The pills are a mother, but better, ...
Yes, I admit
it has gotten to be a bit of a habit ...
I like them more than I like me.
It's a kind of marriage.

(Sexton, 1966/1999f, p. 165)

Sexton wrote many poems that articulated the fantasies driving her addiction. But she also wrote extensively about the fantasies that fueled the obsession with her own death, which she characterized as an addiction. In the posthumously published "Words for Dr. Y," she wrote:

Death,
I need my little addiction to you.
need that tiny voice who,
even as I rise from the sea,
all woman, all there,
says kill me, kill me ...

(Sexton, 1978, p. 4)

Nevertheless, the idea that drugs could relieve her personal suffering kept Sexton fighting to stay alive for much of her life. In "The Addict," she confessed:

I'm on a diet from death ...
It's a kind of war where I plant bombs inside
of myself.
Yes
I try
to kill myself in small amounts,
an innocuous occupation.
Actually I'm hung up on it ...
Eating my eight loaves in a row
and in a certain order as in
the laying on of hands
or the black sacrament.
It's a ceremony ...
Then I lie on my altar
elevated by the eight chemical kisses ...

(Sexton, 1966/1999f, p. 165)

Sexton wrote "Wanting to Die," a poem that articulates the "unnameable lust" she experienced in her previous two suicide attempts, the urge to consume the "magic" of "the enemy."

She addressed the addictive nature of her suicidal urges, which she personified as magic:

> Since you ask, most days I cannot remember.
> I walk in my clothing, unmarked by that voyage.
> Then the almost unnameable lust returns.
> Even then I have nothing against life ...
> But suicides have a special language.
> Like carpenters they want to know *which tools*.
> They never ask *why build*.
> Twice I have so simply declared myself,
> have possessed the enemy, eaten the enemy,
> have taken on his craft, his magic.
> (Sexton, 1964/1999l, pp. 142–143)

As much as Sexton tried – the years of psychoanalytic treatment, the mountains of psychotropic medications, the intoxication of alcohol and pills, and the great hope she invested in her poetry – she ultimately could not outrun the force of Thanatos, as "The Poet of Ignorance" illustrates:

> There is an animal inside me,
> clutching fast to my heart,
> a huge crab.
> The doctors of Boston
> have thrown up their hands.
> They have tried scalpels,
> needles, poison gasses and the like.
> The crab remains.
> It is a great weight.
> I try to forget it, go about my business,
> cook the broccoli, open the shut books,
> brush my teeth and tie my shoes.
> I have tried prayer
> but as I pray the crab grips harder
> and the pain enlarges.
> (Sexton, 1975/1999i, p. 434)

Despite the darkness she viewed as potentiating her gift as a poet, Sexton continued to see the light her writing shone upon her life until the tail end of her career. Even in the throes of suicidal urges, Sexton lived through her poetry. When considering whether to "pull the plug," she relied on her writing for continued life. Consider the following lines from "Live," the final poem in *Live or Die*, for which she won the Pulitzer Prize.

> Here,
> all along,
> thinking I was a killer,
> anointing myself daily
> with my little poisons.
> But no.
> I'm an empress.
> I wear an apron.
> My typewriter writes.
> It didn't break the way it warned.
>   (Sexton, 1966/1999e, p. 169)

Clearly, calling herself "God," a "queen," and an "empress" in her poetry demonstrates the power of her omnipotent fantasies, yet these fantasies were insufficient to sustain her life instinct. In *The Awful Rowing Toward God,* the final work published before her death, Sexton expressed her unrelenting desire for eradication, the potent fantasy to vanish from existence. Although she was famous for crediting her poetry with saving her life, Sexton viewed suicide as the ultimate salvation. She associated her death with vivid images of reaching a place of solace and relief – a place where she could finally squeeze the life from "the gnawing pestilent rat" inside her. In "The Rowing," the opening poem of the volume, she wrote:

> I am rowing, I am rowing
> though the oarlocks stick and are rusty
> and the sea blinks and rolls
> like a worried eyeball,
> but I am rowing, I am rowing,
> though the wind pushes me back
> and I know that that island will not be perfect,
> it will have the flaws of life,
> the absurdities of the dinner table,
> but there will be a door
> and I will open it
> and I will get rid of the rat inside of me,
> the gnawing pestilential rat.
> God will take it with his two hands
> and embrace it.
>   (Sexton, 1975/1999j, pp. 417–418)

Conclusion

The descent from the extremes of highs to the depths of her lows became intolerable for Sexton. Symbolically, she experienced her failures as undercurrents pulling her closer toward death, lamenting that neither her words nor her chemical concoctions stood a chance once faced with the monstrous shadow of her suicidal impulses.

In 1974, at the age of 45, Sexton committed suicide. She died of carbon monoxide poisoning, parked in the garage in the front seat of her red Cougar, wrapped in her mother's old fur coat and clutching a glass of vodka. The push and pull of omnipotent fantasies propelling Sexton toward both self-preservation and self-destruction had finally come to an end. In the eulogy given by Denise Levertov at Sexton's memorial service, she urged her mourners to choose life: "We who are alive must make clear, as she could not, the distinction between creativity and self-destruction" (Levertov, 1981, p. 54).

Chapter 5

The monsters of Stephen King

> We are talking about words ... but you'd do well to remember that we are also talking about magic.
>
> Stephen King

The fears that pervade Stephen King's fantasy life reveal why he is the undisputed master of the modern horror story. "I'm afraid of everything!" he has said outright (Rogak, 2008, p. 1): spiders, snakes, insects, the dark, and death, and that's just for starters. He also harbors superstitions and engages in obsessive-compulsive rituals. King has battled his demons with stories since he was a child. He is renowned for his uncanny ability to strike terror in the heart and keep people reading long after they promised themselves to put the book down.

Since his first novel *Carrie* in 1973, King has been fervently cranking out his own brand of horror, suspense, psychodrama, science fiction, and fantasy. He has written and published more than 65 novels in 38 years, in addition to short stories, articles, book adaptation manuscripts, and works of nonfiction. In 2000, King published a colorful blend of personal insight, humor, and tragedy in a memoir chronicling the experiences that shaped him as a person and a writer. He described *On Writing: A Memoir of the Craft* as "a kind of curriculum vitae – my attempt to show how one writer was formed" (King, 2000, p. 18). This chapter explores the link between King's creativity and narcissistic illusions and examines how those very aspects of mental life made him prone to life-threatening substance abuse problems. An in-depth analysis of King's classic novel *The Shining*, a book King maintains he wrote about himself while unaware that he was doing so, looks at the connection between creativity and addiction. King claimed he was "screaming for help in the only way [he] knew how; through [his] fiction and through [his] monsters" (King, 2000, p. 96).

Fantasy and spell casting

Long before he developed the ability to weave spellbinding tales, King was changing the world around him through the power of his imagination. Reflecting on his earliest memory, King says he imagined being someone else.

Specifically, at about age three, he fantasized that he was the Ringling Brothers Circus Strongboy (King, 2000). In the privacy of his inner world, King found himself in an animal-skin singlet at the center of a vast crowd waiting on the edge of their seats in tense silence. As the spotlight followed his every move, he lifted a cement cinderblock and carried it across the garage that served as center stage. King reflected on the awestruck crowd and how his circus stunt played out in this vivid fantasy:

> Their wondering faces told the story: never had they seen such an incredibly strong kid. "And he's only *two!*" someone muttered in disbelief ... Unknown to me, wasps had constructed a small nest in the lower half of the cinderblock. One of them ... flew out and stung me on the ear. The pain was brilliant, like a poisonous inspiration. It was the worst pain I had ever suffered in my short life, but it only held the top spot for a few seconds. When I dropped the cinderblock on one bare foot, mashing all five toes, I forgot all about the wasp.
>
> (King, 2000, pp. 18–19)

King's first experience of blunting one pain with another was an accident, but that pattern would repeat itself in the future. Moreover, he had an "overactive mind" even as a young child: "My imagination was too big for my head ... so I spent a lot of miserable hours ... [I] couldn't switch off the images once ... [I'd] triggered them" (cited in Rogak, 2008, p. 18). He later attributed the vividness of these images and the power they wield in his fiction to the absence of an internal filter (King, 2000). To compound King's naturally sensitive temperament, his narcissistic illusions of wielding control over the external world were dealt a hard blow at an early age.

When King was only two, his father went out for a pack of cigarettes and stepped out of his life forever. Donald King had landed himself in severe debt and decided to walk out on his wife, Ruth Pillsbury King, and two boys, Stephen and four-year-old Dave. From that point on, the family only referred to Donald as "Daddy Done," short for "Daddy Done Left." King was once asked about having grown up without a father during an interview for the BBC. Rogak (2008, p. 7) described King's startled reaction to the inquiry, giving life to the emotional response she observed:

> Things got painfully intimate, revealing the hurt, petulant boy that still exists close to the surface beneath Stephen King's skin. At that point, his face crumpled a little, he distractedly ran a hand through his hair, and he looked away from the camera, which remained focused on him for a second or two before abruptly cutting away.

Not long after incurring the loss of his father, King found himself disturbed yet oddly fascinated by stories in the news following the rampage of a notorious serial killer. During an interview for *60 Minutes*, the writer recalled his childhood fascination with the serial killer and the recognition that the "empty" quality in the serial killer was something he found in himself:

> To me, Charles Starkweather was totally empty. I was examining the human equivalent of a black hole, and that's what really attracted me to Starkweather ... You could see it in his eyes, to a degree. There was something gone in there. But I also understood that it was in me, and it was in a lot of people.
>
> (King, 1997)

As a child, King watched a movie called *The Snake Pit* in which a woman is driven insane after finding herself in an asylum with no idea of how or why she ended up there. The movie infected him with the deeply troubling belief that "you can go insane quite easily" (Rogak, 2008, p. 16). Ironically, around the age of eight, he became infatuated with anything that could strike a sense of terror in his heart and began to suffer sleep disturbances (King, 2000). In one childhood recurring nightmare he saw the body of a man hanging from a scaffold at the top of a hill. "When the wind caused the corpse to turn in the air, I saw that it was my own face, rotted and picked by the birds, but still obviously mine. And then the corpse opened its eyes and looked at me" (Spignesi, 1991, p. 19). As the nightmares continued, King began to feel that he himself was becoming the very monsters he feared the most.

Perhaps King's unconscious identification with his father played out in the author's dreams. Perhaps in an effort to shield himself from the pain inflicted by his absent father, King internalized the feelings of rejection associated with his father and sought to identify with these bad experiences of self as a means to controlling them (Fairbairn, 1952). Following Fairbairn's theories, we can speculate that rather than deal with the pain of being rejected, King placed the blame for his father's absence on his own "badness." In other words, he was purchasing stability in the external world at the price of sacrificing internal peace of mind (Fairbairn, 1952). In an effort to put these ideas to words, the unconscious realm of his mind may have sounded something like this: *It's not my father who is bad ... it was actually my own badness that drove him away. I am the one responsible for my father's leaving. He abandoned me because I am bad.*

In the wake of Donald's abrupt exit, Ruth King was forced to move her two sons around, enlisting the help of family members so she could work two and three jobs to support her children and pay off the debt her husband had left behind. While his mother worked around the clock and his older brother spent time with kids his own age, King ended up spending much of his childhood alone. In response to questions about the influence his solitude had on his writing, King remarked: "As a kid, I didn't talk much, I wrote ... I'm not a very good talker. I'm not used to externalizing my thoughts other than

on paper, which is typical of writers" (Rogak, 2008, p. 100). A close childhood friend of King's expressed his belief that the author's sense of isolation
was a significant influence on his writing. "Steve spent a lot of time by himself ... he was different from many of us who knew him because he was more
isolated than we were" (p. 58).

King also spent a great deal of time home sick from school, suffering repeated bouts of the measles, strep throat, and ear infections during the first grade.
To pass the time, he became an avid reader and spent the majority of one year
immersed in "approximately six tons of comic books" from which he then
progressed to Tom Swift and Jack London novels. When his nose wasn't buried
in a novel or comic book, King was listening to Ray Bradbury's science-fiction
stories on the radio or watching horror movies. "I liked to be scared, I liked the
total surrender of emotional control," he confessed (Rogak, 2008, p. 16). To
articulate the pleasure that the horror genre induced in him, King explained his
need to feel afraid as striving, on some level, to achieve mastery over those
things that terrify him most, not unlike the phenomenon Freud described as
repetition compulsion (Freud, 1955a/1920). For the emerging young writer,
books were "a uniquely portable magic" (King, 2000, p. 96).

While growing up, King's fertile imagination served as an increasingly
refined tool for him in carving out a future career as a writer. In the wake of
his father's abandonment, King's fantasy life – frightening as it was – may
have seemed a refuge from a cold and unforgiving external world while
simultaneously mirroring it. Ironically, the young King immersed himself in
stories of horror and fear in an effort to cope with the horror and fear he
faced in his life. Part of his love for the thrill of being afraid was the exertion
of a sense of omnipotent control over his reality by seeing the worst pain in
his life pale in comparison to the traumas of his stories. He said: "I've always
believed if you think the very worst, then, no matter how bad things get (and
in my heart I've always been convinced that they can get pretty bad), they'll
never get as bad as *that*" (King, 2000, p. 234).

It was this love of horror stories and the protection they provided him that
first sparked King's inspiration to create his own stories. For him writing was
his most powerful remedy and defense against the emotional discomfort in his
life (Rogak, 2008). In his nonfiction work *Danse Macabre*, King (1981, p. 13)
provided insight into the reasons his life became devoted to creating horror
stories when there is already so much *real* horror in the world:

> We make up horror to help us cope with the real [stories]. The dream of
> horror is in itself an out-letting and a lancing ... and it may well be that
> the mass-media dream of horror can sometimes become a nationwide
> analyst's couch ... People often ask me to parse out meaning from my
> stories, to relate them back to my life. I'm always puzzled to realize years
> later that in some ways I was delineating my own problems, and per-
> forming a kind of self-psychoanalysis.

King's Oedipal drama

As King entered adolescence and became more curious about his father, he rummaged around in his aunt's attic one day, where his mother had stored the packed artifacts left behind by his father. In one of the biggest surprises of his life, King stumbled on a box of 1940s science-fiction novels, along with a stack of rejection slips from magazines with hastily scribbled notes of encouragement asking Donald to try again. His father had been an aspiring writer too! In *Danse Macabre*, King (1981, p. 97) speculated about whether his initial infatuation with creative writing and fiction could be partially attributed to this moment when he discovered the interests he and his father shared in common:

> Talent is only a compass, and we'll not discuss why it points toward magnetic north; instead we'll treat briefly of that moment when the needle actually swings toward that great point of attraction. It has always seemed peculiar to me that I owe that moment in my own life to my father, who left my mother when I was two and my brother, David, four.

King might have unconsciously fantasized about becoming merged, reunited perhaps, with the idealized image of his father. King himself has said, "I am always interested in the idea that a lot of fiction writers write for their fathers because their fathers are gone ... There does seem to be a target that this stuff pours out toward" (Platt, 1983, p. 278). On the other hand, the more aggressive, powerful, and protected aspect of King's personality argued against expressing such vulnerabilities. The opposing sides clashed, and King expressed his bitter conflict: "Maybe in some sort of imaginative way I'm searching for him or maybe that's just a lot of horseshit" (p. 278).

The young King learned that writing might help him bury the haunting memories of his father, and this added further fuel to the fire of his creative drive. One of the rare instances in which Ruth King discussed her ex-husband with her son came after King happened upon his father's literary remnants. She told her son that his father had given up on everything he ever tried due to laziness. King thanked his mother for her honesty and then raced up the stairs to his bedroom where his typewriter awaited (Rogak, 2008). This sudden spurt of creative inspiration may have been propelled by omnipotent fantasies in which King slew his father with the power of his words and stepped over the body to achieve the literary success Dad never could – an Oedipal victory. In succeeding where his father had failed, King would forever win the admiration of his mother, thus enhancing his victory over his father. Perhaps the intensity of his creative pursuits partially reflects an expression of rage toward his father over his abandonment as well as furious competitive strivings to be the sole winner of his mother's love. In becoming his mother's ideal son, King could save her by filling the position of her absent husband and becoming the man his father never could be. King's drive to succeed as a writer and to have his work revered by others was seemingly insatiable. Succeeding would symbolically show his father (in fantasy) that he was more powerful than he and could destroy him. Through his writing, King expresses not only the pain of losing his father and his unconscious desire to connect with this shadowy figure, but also his rage, hatred, and a sense of mastery over the dark world his father left behind.

King now began working feverishly to purge the badness inside of him with a fresh sheet of paper. "I'd be upstairs during the summer pounding away in my underpants, streaming with sweat," King recalled (as cited in Rogak, 2008, p. 23). He typed so aggressively that he broke the M key off his typewriter and later went back and filled in by hand all of the missing letter M's on the pages (King, 2000).

While the memory of King's father lived in a dark place where narcissistic illusions warred with damaged self-esteem, he internalized his mother's presence as a guiding light, shining through the fog of his pain. King's perspective is not uncommon in families where there is an absent parent, especially one that is viewed as "bad"; children inevitably develop fierce loyalty to the remaining parental figure. The author found inspiration for his writing through maternal mirroring, idealization, and warmth. Ruth's parenting gratified her son's narcissistic illusions. Not only did King receive a sense of being special, unique, and gifted in return for presenting his mother with one of his stories (Rogak, 2008); he was also given the power to communicate something crucial to her through his writing. Perhaps King was trying to tell his mother that he would always be there for her, that he would protect her and lavish her with the gifts of his creativity. He would not only correct his father's failure to succeed as a writer; he would also mend the wounds of the man's painful disappearance. King would never be the coward who ran away from the pressures of raising a family.

As the muse for his creative writing, Ruth became a strong support for King's triumphant rise over the significant losses of his early life. Her mirroring provided the empathy and encouragement that allowed her son to transform his omnipotent fantasies into creative productions, later to be treasured by millions of fans. King (2000, p. 28) said:

> Eventually I showed one of these [stories] to my mother, and she was charmed. I remember her slightly amazed smile, as if she was unable to believe a kid of hers could be so smart. Practically a damned prodigy, for God's sake. I had never seen that look on her face before. Not on my account, anyway. And I absolutely loved it.

King reports that his mother often served as an unwavering source of energy for his writing projects, adamantly expressing her faith in his talents throughout his life. Reflecting on how his mother's belief in him gave him the courage to pursue his literary ambitions, King said, "Writing is a lonely job. Having someone who believes in you makes a lot of difference. They don't have to make speeches. Just believing is usually enough" (King, 2000, p. 73). As extra incentive, Ruth paid her son a small fee to read some of his earliest stories. When King first pondered being able to write as a career – to actually be paid to do what he loved most – he experienced "an immense feeling of possibility … as if I had been ushered into a vast building filled with closed doors and had been given leave to open any one I liked. There were more doors than one person could ever open in a lifetime, I thought" (p. 26).

During his freshman year of college, while adjusting to living away from home, King wrote his first novel and sold his first short story to a pulp magazine for $35. According to his college roommate, "When he sat down at a typewriter, he would just go. He was so incredibly focused that if you hit him with a brick, he wouldn't notice" (Rogak, 2008, p. 46). Similarly, his freshman English professor remarked, "Steve was religious about writing, and he wrote continuously, diligently. He created his own world" (p. 41). Finding meaning in a deep love for the craft of weaving a tale, King set out on an all-consuming personal journey. Reflecting on the magical function his creativity served for him throughout his life, he said, "Writing is magic, as much the water of life as any other creative art. The water is free. So drink. Drink and be filled up" (King, 2000, p. 270).

Considering the ways that King's writing gratified omnipotent fantasies from an early age, it is not surprising to learn that he regards his impulse to write as an addiction. He once joked about his writing talent as being the result of an addiction gene he'd inherited from his mother that "got rewired somewhere along the way" (Rogak, 2008, p. 156). King suggested, "it's part of that obsessive deal that makes you a writer in the first place, that makes you want to write it all down. Writing is an addiction for me. Even when the writing is not going well, if I don't do it, the fact that I'm not doing it nags at me" (as cited in Rogak, 2008, p. 2). For King, writing and substances were both portals to nurturing and expressing his omnipotent fantasies. Like his writing, his use of substances provided him with the intense satisfaction of feeling "filled up." But as King soon found out, the void he was seeking to fill through both his writing and his substance abuse was more cavernous than he had anticipated.

Scribbler's little helpers: substance abuse and narcissistic illusion

King began using drugs when he was about 17, a pattern that would continue for approximately 30 years. Like the fantasies of fiction, drugs presented a transformational solution for life's many problems. But as King's relationship with alcohol and other drugs progressed, what once seemed an innocently tantalizing remedy became a virulent disease. King picked up his first drink during the late 1960s in his senior year of high school and found himself instantly hooked, which probably indicates a genetic element of causation. He fell in love with alcohol's ability to modify the textures of his consciousness, providing him with the illusion of escaping his body and slowing the frantic pace of his mind. He described his initial experience of intoxication as a "vague sense of roaring goodwill" (King, 2000, p. 89). Alcohol provided "a clearer sense that most of your consciousness is out of your body, hovering like a camera in a science fiction movie and filming everything" (p. 89). Commenting on his own propensity for addictive behaviors, King recounted a story his mother once told him about a peculiar craving she experienced while pregnant with him. She would go out to the road and pull up a piece of tar to chew on. King says, "There was something in that tar, that, she, I, needed" (as cited in Rogak, 2008, p. 156). King facetiously speculated that it was his mother's tar consumption that spawned his own proclivity for drugs and alcohol (Rogak, 2008).

While attending college during the late 1960s, King continued to drink excessively and began using harder drugs available on college campuses across America. "I did a lot of LSD and peyote and mescaline, more than sixty trips in all," he said (Rogak, 2008, p. 45). One of King's old roommates told a story about how Stephen and his friends took a hallucinatory drug known for its potency and equilibrium-disturbing effects. That night, everyone became lost in the experience of talking, laughing, and listening to music. Suddenly, one of the roommates noticed that King had disappeared. After frantically searching the house and then heading to campus to check the bars, the dorms, and even the English department, King's roommates found him. One friend recalled:

> He was sitting in a three-legged easy chair with his feet up on a cranking kerosene heater, which was in the process of melting his rubber boots, and he was oblivious to it all … I think he was reading *Psycho*. On this particular drug, no one else could even manage to turn the pages, but Steve was sitting there reading, totally safe in his own little cocoon of fiction.
>
> (Rogak, 2008, p. 46)

By the time he was finishing college, King was married and having children. He was teaching English just to scrape by in supporting his family, while writing late into the night, fueled by his ambition to succeed as a novelist. King was terrified of failing as a writer, following in the footsteps of his father. As the stress of his life increased, so too did his drinking. It was around this period of time that King also began occasionally experimenting with cocaine. King's initial use of cocaine most likely added fuel to the fire that had been burning inside him since childhood. "With cocaine, one snort, and it owned me body and soul," King once said. "It was like the missing link. Cocaine was my on switch, and it seemed like a really good energizing drug. You try some and think, 'Wow, why haven't I been taking this for years?'" (Rogak, 2008, p. 96). Gradually, King became enraptured by fantasies of the power in alcohol and cocaine and their perceived effect on his creativity and ability to crank ink onto paper.

Nevertheless, King soon discovered that the powers of intoxication could not protect him from everything. At the age of 27, the King family was celebrating the financial success of his first published novel, *Carrie*. But King's momentary relief from his greatest fears was short-lived, cut short by his mother's cancer diagnosis in 1973. Shortly after *Carrie*'s release, Nellie Ruth died of uterine cancer. During her final days, her sister (King's aunt) sat beside her, reading *Carrie* front to back aloud to her. In King's memoir, he suggests that the death of his mother was one of the major factors that propelled his drinking habits to the next level. Lamenting Ruth's burial service, King wrote, "I gave the eulogy. I think I did a pretty good job, considering how drunk I was" (2000, p. 94). With his mother gone, and bouts of grief-induced depression looming overhead, King found himself diving deeper into the bottle. And with more alcohol came more frequent encounters with uppers like cocaine and downers like Valium, chemicals that were soon to become essentials to his ritualistic writing cocktails.

In *On Writing*, King described the state of mind in which he composed some of his most notoriously spine-tingling novels. King recounted writing *The Tommyknockers*, during which he frequently worked until midnight with his heart pounding and cotton swabs stuck up his nose "to stem the coke-induced bleeding" (p. 97). On a number of occasions, King's wife, Tabitha, emerged from her bedroom in the morning to find her husband passed out on the floor beside his writing desk in a pool of his own vomit. As the substances King abused took their toll, even his seemingly immortal creativity gradually began to suffer. While he found himself unable to stop drinking and using drugs, he began to lament the complete loss of his sober mind as well as his emotional connection to his novels.

> At the end of my adventures I was drinking a case of sixteen-ounce tall-boys a night, and there's one novel, *Cujo*, that I barely remember writing at all. I don't say that with pride or shame, only with a vague sense of sorrow and loss. I like that book. I wish I could remember enjoying the good parts as I put them down on the page.
>
> (King, 2000, p. 99)

King's addictions ultimately led to his feeling that he had been evicted from life. He no longer wanted to drink but he no longer wanted to be sober either. His family and friends decided to intervene, and his wife, Tabitha, gave him an ultimatum, which ruled out the possibility of his continuing to drink and drug while living in the house with her and the kids (King, 2000). With this, King faced the realization that he might've forgotten what it was like to be sober. "What would happen to me without dope? I had forgotten the trick of being straight" (p. 96). The question that had loomed over Stephen King's head for years finally came crashing down upon him along with the ultimatum: Would he still be able to write if he gave up alcohol and drugs? He was terrified that if he stopped using substances, he would be left without the rocket fuel he needed to be successful as a writer. Ultimately, he decided he could no longer risk losing his family, and gave up all drugs and alcohol by the late 1980s.

In early sobriety, King was horrified to find that his greatest fears were coming true while attempting to write under the deafening silence of his newly sober mind. "He couldn't. The words wouldn't come, his sentences were complete gibberish, and each letter might as well have been a hieroglyph" (Rogak, 2008, p. 159). Although this period of time was relatively quiet for King with regard to producing work for publication, he soon rediscovered the inner voice that had shaped his fiction for so many years and returned to his normal level of productivity. King realized that he no longer needed his chemical companions to write stories and has since written some of his most popular and beloved works, including *Dolores Claiborne, The Green Mile,* and the epic *Dark Tower* series. Looking back on his fears that giving up substances would extinguish his creative writing capabilities, King found it easier to see the wall of rationalization he had been carefully constructing around himself:

> Alcoholics build defenses like the Dutch build dikes. I spent the first twelve years or so of my married life assuring myself that I "just liked to drink." I also employed the world-famous Hemingway Defense. Although never clearly articulated (it would not be manly to do so), the Hemingway Defense goes something like this: as a writer, I am a very sensitive fellow, but I am also a man, and real men don't give in to their sensitivities. Only *sissy*-men do that. Therefore I drink. How else can I face the existential horror of it all and continue to work?
>
> (King, 2000, pp. 93–96)

Looking back on the progression of his addiction after more than a decade of sobriety, King has reflected on the link between the suppression of growing concerns about his addictions and the characters that came alive in his earliest novels. For example, King (2000) cited *Misery* as one novel into which he spun his growing desperation about cocaine's hold over him into a tale of a writer held captive by an adoring, psychotic fan. The psychopath, Annie, uses various means of violence and torture to coerce her favorite author, Paul Sheldon, into writing the stories the way she wants them to be. Commenting on Annie as the metaphorical villain, King said, "Annie was coke, Annie was booze, and I decided I was tired of being Annie's pet writer ... I was afraid that I wouldn't be able to work anymore if I quit drinking and drugging" (p. 98).

More than any other novel, King marks *The Shining* as the most blatant representation of how his innermost demons were surfacing in his writing at the time. It was through the story's main protagonist, Jack Torrence, that King voiced his first cries for help as an addict. He could not ask for help directly from friends and family; he could handle his problems on his own because "a real man always can" (King, 2000, pp. 93–96). So, instead, King began to scream for help in the only way he knew how, "through my fiction and through my monsters" (p. 96). Reflecting back on this time, King wrote:

> *Holy shit, I'm an alcoholic*, I thought, and there was no dissenting opinion from inside my head – I was, after all, the guy who had written *The Shining* without even realizing (at least until that night) that I was writing about myself.
>
> (King, 2000, p. 95)

A closer look at *The Shining* as it relates to King's fantasy life reveals further ties between his creative energies and his substance abuse.

House of mirrors

The Shining (King, 1977) best articulates the force of narcissistic illusions driving both King's creative writing and substance abuse. Jack Torrence, the novel's main protagonist, has been called an "amalgam of King's personal fears at the turning point of his career" (Winter, 1984, p. 48). Torrence is terrified of failing as a writer, as well as losing his family due to his increasingly destructive alcohol use. And while King was on track to achieving a highly successful career as a novelist with the launching of his first two published novels at the time he was writing *The Shining,* he held fiercely to beliefs that he would soon awaken from the surrealist dream he was living – to the extent that he fought extensively with Tabitha about spending any of the money that was pouring in from his initial successes. What if his next novel failed? What if the magic well of his creativity ran dry? The more King spent his days drunk and afraid that failure was still a very real threat, the more anger and resentment he felt toward his wife and even his son. He became terrified of the emergence of true feelings of rage toward his three-year-old son – terrified of the mere existence within him of such capacities for anger toward his child. King used these fears to create Jack's character, and the vicious circle in the book that paralleled his own. Torrence is teaching high school English to scrape by and has developed a serious drinking habit. The more he feels that his writing career will fail, the tighter alcohol grips him, and, in turn, the scarier his anger toward his family grows. The novel serves as a rich illustration of how King's creativity and substance abuse were both fueled by fantasies of wielding omnipotent control over his life and his closest relationships.

When the first words of *The Shining* began appearing on paper, the world King had fashioned in his effort to maintain omnipotent control was suddenly shaken like a snow globe. He was still struggling with his mother's death. His addiction was worsening. He may not have known he was writing an extraordinary novel, but he did know the turmoil in his life was becoming unmanageable. Narcissistic illusions of being imbued with omnipotent powers, encouraged by his idealizing mother, had incited King's creativity from an early age. Although she was gone, her internal presence burned all the brighter. The internalized voice of his mother guided him in the process of writing and took the edge off his fears: "It was like, if I write this, it won't happen, like I'm trying to keep the hex off," he recalled (Rogak, 2008, p. 79).

King's unconscious fantasies may have sounded something like this: *Mom always said that talking about my fears is the best way to make them go away ... Maybe* writing *about the things I fear the most will also make them go away. I'm good when I write, she showed me that. I can write away the bad, I can reassert the good. I can save myself and the people I love.* King (2000) described how his writing has served as a kind of "psychological protection" for him: "It's like drawing a magic circle around myself and my family. If you write a novel where the bogeyman gets somebody else's children, maybe they'll never get your own children," he has said (p. 234). Exactly. Think about the terrible things that happen to Jack and his family in *The Shining*, and it's easy to see how the author was magically warding off catastrophic consequences in his own life: the possibility of not being able to write, even though he had already experienced success; madness, violence, abandonment, and the loss of those he most deeply loved. This is omnipotent fantasy and narcissistic illusion at its most poignant.

As King's narcissistic illusions waned in his waking life, his omnipotent fantasies about the magical powers of alcohol and drugs intensified. Rather than verbalize his concerns to others through direct speech, King began to communicate his fears indirectly by putting his feelings into words with Torrence's help:

> He [Torrence] was still an alcoholic, always would be ... It had nothing to do with willpower, or the morality of drinking, or the weakness or strength of his own character. There was a broken switch somewhere inside, or a circuit breaker that didn't work, and he had been propelled down the chute willynilly, slowly at first, then accelerating as [his job at] Stovington [High School] applied its pressures on him.
>
> (King, 1977, p. 73)

As King was losing his grip over his use of alcohol and drugs, he felt himself transforming into his father – inadequate, spineless – a true failure. When asked during an interview if the ghosts in *The Shining* are real or just a figment of Torrence's imagination, King once responded: "Torrence himself is a haunted house. He's haunted by his father. It pops up again, and again, and again" (Underwood & Miller, 1989, p. 105). While conceiving the Torrence family triangle – Jack, his wife, Wendy, and their son, Danny – King identified his own rage and fear as the driving forces behind the novel's inspiration. Through Torrence, he strove to put his "dark passenger" to rest. Yet, in the novel, Torrence is repeatedly haunted by memories of breaking his son's arm after losing his temper. In a frightening revelation, Jack Torrence recognizes that he is becoming the same person as his father. He reflects on the displacement of his anger and the roots of his rage toward his son, Danny:

> And [Jack's] temper … All his life he had been trying unsuccessfully to control it. He could remember himself at seven … He had gone out and hurled a rock at a passing car. His father had seen that, and he had descended on little Jacky, roaring. He had reddened Jack's behind … and then blackened his eye. And when his father had gone into the house, muttering, to see what was on television, Jack had come upon a stray dog and had kicked it into the gutter.
>
> (King, 1977, p. 122)

King's festering anger had begun to frighten him on an all-too-regular basis, especially when it came to his relationship with his son. Reflecting on how unsettling it was to confront the aggression he felt toward his children, King explained how the creation of fictional stories offered him psychological protection from his most painful personal truths (Beahm, 1989). For instance, he once credited a reason for his success to his need to hide from that which he felt he should confess through his writing. King described feeling "horrified" by his own feelings of violence toward his children, adding that he was able to "vomit" his most aggressive energies out into his writing (Beahm, 1989, p. 36).

Once again, we discern the spell of omnipotent fantasy: *If Jack breaks his son's arm and goes crazy, then I won't do those things. I will project the evil in me and contain and isolate it in my story, the magic circle. If Jack fails, I will succeed. He will be my unbearable doppelgänger.*

King candidly recalled the day when his three-year-old son, Joe, got his hands on one of his manuscripts and tried his hand at the family trade. When King discovered the pages had been scribbled over in Crayola crayon, he thought, "The little son of a bitch, I could kill him." King goes on to confess, "I had feelings of anger about my kids that I never expected. I felt hostile [toward them]. I wanted to grab them and hit them … I felt guilty feelings because of my brutal impulses" (Rogak, 2008, p. 78). It was during that time that he wrote the following passage in *The Shining*:

> When [Jack Torrence] went back into his study and saw Danny [his five-year-old son] standing there, wearing nothing but his training pants and a

grin, a slow, red cloud of rage had eclipsed Jack's reason ... He had been drinking beer and doing the Act II corrections when Wendy said the phone was for him, and Danny had poured the can of beer all over the pages... He had whirled Danny around to spank him, his big adult fingers digging into the scant meat of the boy's forearm, meeting around it in a closed fist, and the snap of the breaking bone had not been loud ... HUGE, but not loud. Just enough of a sound to slit through the red fog like an arrow – but instead of letting in sunlight, that sound let in the dark clouds of shame and remorse, the terror, the agonizing convulsion of the spirit.

(King, 1977, p. 13)

King's aggressive fantasies found an additional outlet in Jack Torrence's dreams. Jack remembers a traumatic scene from his childhood involving his parents, and, for the first time, the reader receives a clear message about the extent to which Jack's unconscious mind is haunted by the lingering ghost of his father.

Love began to curdle at nine, when his father put his mother into the hospital with his cane. He had begun to carry the cane a year earlier, when a car accident had left him lame. After that he was never without it, long and black and thick and gold-headed. Now, dozing, Jack's body twitched in a remembered cringe at the sound it made in the air, a murderous swish, and its heavy crack against the wall ... or against flesh. He had beaten their mother for no good reason at all, suddenly and without warning.

(King, 1977, p. 152)

With the residue of these haunting memories still in his head, Jack descends into a restless sleep, laden with additional disturbing dreams steeped in childhood memories. Jack dreams that he is scrolling through channels on the hotel's CB radio. Suddenly, a chillingly familiar voice comes crackling through the speaker – that of his long-deceased father:

Kill [Danny]. You have to kill him, Jacky, and [Wendy], too. Because a real artist must suffer. Because each man kills the thing he loves. Because they'll always be conspiring against you, trying to hold you back and drag you down. Right this minute that boy of yours is in where he shouldn't be. Trespassing. That's what he's doing. He's a goddamn little pup. Cane him for it, Jacky, cane him within an inch of his life. Have a drink Jacky my boy ... Then I'll go with you while you give him his medicine. I know you can do it, of course you can. You must kill him. You have to kill him, Jacky, and her, too.

(King, 1977, p. 155)

In one interpretation of Jack's nightmare, the violent impulses he experiences toward Danny and Wendy are a reflection of the *badness* he has internalized in response to his own father. One may wonder what, specifically, about the nature of this dream is so dreadful and yet so compelling? Readers identify on some level with Jack's identification with and willingness to embody the badness he associates with the memory of his father. In tapping into unconscious dimensions of human relatedness, King stirs the same sleeping beast in the hearts of readers. King himself said that he felt a sense of relief from writing stories like *The Shining* because the psychological conditions of the characters are so close to home (Rogak, 2008). The way King highlights the human aspects of the murderous monster that Jack Torrence becomes is a powerful literary achievement. King's omnipotent fantasies led the way in creating *The Shining*, whispering that if he experienced his greatest fears through the characters in his fiction – those of being unable to control his rage toward his son, of being abandoned by his family, and being doomed to a life of alcoholic misery and squalor – he would never have to live them out in reality. Through these fantasies, he achieved a sense of omnipotent control over the world around him. But by transposing these very real personal fears and troubles, King was also subtly endearing his readers to his characters. In doing so, he allied readers with the story's bloodthirsty – yet undeniably human – monster and essentially placed them in the accomplice seat. As the novel nears its dark and chaotic finale, readers don't just simply observe Jack's insanity; they feel it. Thus, the character of Jack Torrence is a chillingly poignant illustration of how King's fears were transposed into the hearts of millions of fans. Through his narcissistic illusions of gaining a sense of mastery and control over the badness inside him, he produced what might be his best work. Moreover, he succeeded in mastering his readers by capturing their undivided attention while they read his compelling tale. With the good maternal voice helping him craft the bad impulses associated with the internal representation of his father into a chilling story, King created this unforgettable novel.

King's efforts to achieve mastery over his deepest fears resulted in both the creation of his most legendary and critically acclaimed novel and almost precipitated his self-destruction. His writing and substance abuse offered illusory promises of omnipotent control over himself and the world to take himself out his own skin and make reality the place he needed it to be. King pursued fantasies of transforming who he was, where he was, and what he could do about it. He admitted, "If it would change your consciousness, I was all for it" (Rogak, 2008, p. 157).

Both King's creative energies and substance abuse brought him to life with a euphoric sense of omnipotence, while simultaneously serving as omens of potential disaster. Did he possess the "strength" to function as a successful writer, husband, father, and man while still chasing the seductive thrills and temptations of cocaine and alcohol? Or would his family and talent abandon him as he crawled deeper into his own personally fashioned grave, dug by his addictions?

Writing and drugging protected King from his greatest fears while simultaneously helping him overcome them. Whereas King's writing and substance abuse transformed his world, no amount of words and stories could remove the early wounds he incurred. Omnipotent fantasies provided King with temporary relief from his suffering, but the rebound impact was at times devastating. When he experienced the power of his creative energies waning, his compensatory use of substances escalated. However, this omnipotent formula only worked for a while. In his frantic efforts to outrun his fears, King's focus on his writing became as obsessive as his use of substances. The pangs of withdrawal were just as painful in the face of "writer's block" as those he experienced when attempting to abstain from the drugs. Reflecting on both the healthy and unhealthy aspects of his creative impulses, King said:

> I have a marketable obsession ... The arts are obsessional, and obsession is dangerous. It's like a knife in the mind ... In some cases ... the knife can turn savagely upon the person wielding it. Art is localized illness, usually benign ... [but] sometimes terribly malignant (p. 26) ... I'm able to "write myself sane" as that fine poet Anne Sexton put it. It's an old technique of therapists, you know: get the patient to write out his demons. A Freudian exorcism.
>
> (as cited in Norden, 1983, p. 36)

In emphasizing that writing has been therapeutic and necessary for his sanity, King echoes the voice of Sexton, linking them across a chasm of time and cultures. We have unearthed the narcissistic illusions entertained by both Sexton and King through an examination of their creative writing and their substance abuse. In both cases, we have shown how omnipotent fantasies assumed an addictive quality that shaped their insatiable creative drives and their deepest suffering. For both authors, deeply embedded in these illusions was the conflict between their growth-promoting aspects and self-destructive qualities. When examining the differences between Sexton and King as individuals, we have seen a number of striking parallels in the omnipotent fantasies they entertained throughout their lives. The next section examines in more depth the similarities and differences in the omnipotent projects (and their antecedents) of these two compelling authors.

Parsing King's and Sexton's omnipotent fantasies

Both King and Sexton's creativity served to gratify omnipotent fantasies of maintaining a tie to their rejecting caregiver(s). King's father and Sexton's mother had aspired to be writers themselves. In King's household, he received praise and attention from his mother for every piece of writing he presented to her, and it was known that his father always dreamed of becoming a writer before deserting the family. Likewise, in Sexton's household, writers were praised as representing society's highest tier. Sexton's parents respected, admired, and loved writers. Sexton, on the other hand, never felt fortunate enough to assume such status in her parents' eyes.

From the reports of King and Sexton, we discern that both experienced omnipotent fantasies of establishing the unrequited love of their caregivers through their writing. At the same time, however, their writing became an outlet through which they drained tremendous anger, which was rooted in early narcissistic injuries. In fantasy, the pen served as a sword against their fiercest inner demons – their rejecting caregiver(s). King and Sexton felt they might quell those tormenting inner voices in their writing.

King and Sexton fantasized that the single parent left standing would be *all theirs* after they had destroyed their bad objects with their literary weapons. King could win his mother's heart by rescuing her from the tormenting memory of her evil husband, and Sexton could win her father's love by taking the place of her mother as the family's "most talented woman." In their narcissistic Oedipal illusions, King could consume the undivided love of his mother by becoming the man his father never could be, and Sexton could replace her mother, becoming the sole receiver of her father's love.

While similar in many ways, the nuances of fantasies generated in their early relationships are also a place where King's and Sexton's histories diverge. King often responded to questions about his father's absence by suggesting that he couldn't really miss what was never there (Rogak, 2008). Since the moment his mother first told him that his father had given up on his dreams of becoming a writer, King became attached to his typewriter as if it were another limb. From then on he put every ounce of his energy into creating stories that he fantasized would bring the father he never knew home, while also sending the message that, should he ever return, he would no longer pull rank as "leading male" in the family.

Alternatively, Sexton stopped writing for nearly a decade after the blow she received upon presenting her first poem to her mother. Sexton fantasized about finally gaining the love and acceptance of her mother through poetry. Instead, she ended up feeling more "unwanted" than ever. Only with the encouragement of her psychiatrist, following her first suicide attempt, did Sexton pick up writing again. The concrete, physical presence of Sexton's rejecting parental figure accounted for her decade-long literary cessation. Whereas King most likely felt greater freedom to both fill and outgrow the shoes of a man who existed only in his fantasies, Sexton was threatened by her mother's jealous rage and could not at first continue in her writing pursuits after her mother accused her of plagiarism. Whereas King had no reason to fear that his writing would bring any such repercussions, this message was clear to Sexton: *Mother is the talented female writer in the family … and all those who challenge her will be swiftly dealt with.*

Further, while King's father left the family when King was only two, Sexton's parents were constantly present in her life up until their deaths during the latter part of Sexton's adult life. And yet, while physically present in her life, Sexton's parents both battled substance abuse problems, and her relationship with her parents lacked the love, support, and emotional connection King found with his mother. Sexton felt she had been "spread out daily and examined for flaws" (as cited in Colburn, 1988, p. 231). In contrast, the unwavering support of King's mother blunted the painful early loss of his father. King's mother mirrored her son's creativity, while Sexton's mother viciously competed with her, and her father supported his wife in that regard.

From the narrative analyses of Sexton and King presented here, much has been revealed about the ways in which omnipotent fantasies influenced these writers' style, presentation, and form of creativity. King often sought to disguise and project his deepest and most personal conflicts through his characters, cloaking them in the garb of monsters and tragic heroes. His reader – not he – was the one who was afraid. His horror stories provided the omnipotent illusion that he could *master* and *control* his fears by writing about them. Perhaps he wished to assume the role of the courageous "King" of the horror story, the one who possessed the bravery and strength to go places in the mind that most men feared to tread. He would become the "man of steel" who takes in life's most terrifying truths and challenges his readers with stomach-churning horror, gore, and violence he digests and then spits back out. Through the horrific scenes in his books, King asks his readers, "Are you tough enough to stomach what I'm about to show you? Can you handle the truth?" Similarly, in his memoir he noted:

> If you expect to succeed as a writer, rudeness should be the second-to-least of your concerns. The least of all should be polite society and what it expects. If you intend to write as truthfully as you can, your days as a member of polite society are numbered, anyway.
>
> (King, 2000, p. 205)

Many of his books are exceptionally long – demonstrating his power as a writer, the "king" of horror stories who towers above competitors. One wonders whether narcissistic illusions played some role in his recently outspoken hatred of the e-book – a format where size truly does not matter. Refusing to release his latest publication in e-book format, he proposed instead, "Let people stir their sticks and go to an actual bookstore, rather than a digital one" (King, 2013, para. 2).

Sexton's poetry demonstrates a sense of power parallel to King's fiction, but from a different angle. Like King, she fantasized about sweeping up readers in the dizzying current of her words. Narcissistic illusions of healing herself, changing others, and transforming the world were essential to the forces driving her creativity. Sexton had very little control over the circumstances of her childhood and felt invisible and uncared for by her parents. Thus, she sought to seize omnipotent control through the power of the pen. In contrast to the epic length of King's stories, Sexton's poetry cuts straight to the heart of her intentions. She made no efforts to disguise the meaning of her writing the way King did. In her confessional poetry, she revealed truths about herself, her relationships, and society.

Both King and Sexton relish striking the reader with emotional force, like a slap across the face. King did not easily access his feelings. Even as a child, he loved horror because it helped him to feel *something*. He spent little time exposed to human relationships, hidden away in the confines of his own imagination and the worlds he inhabited through reading and writing. Experiencing terror excited him and made him feel alive. Likewise, Sexton wanted the unbridled truth and the raw honesty of her poetry to shock her readers and breathe life into herself and her audience. Like King, Sexton described her distaste for the sense of "deadness" that imprisoned men and women behind their picket fences, a sterile image of 1960s suburbia, American society's version of the "good life." Sexton attacked the deadening effects of traditional gender roles and was driven by fantasies of achieving unprecedented success with her poetry. For both King and Sexton, narcissistic illusions often materialized; they were both determined and ambitious people, and they both achieved significant success in their lifetime.

King vs. Sexton: omnipotent fantasies, addiction, and recovery

Both King and Sexton described their relentless urge to write as an addiction. This is not surprising, since narcissistic illusions possess an addictive quality (Mitchell, 2000). And while their creative drives brought King and Sexton great success, their omnipotent fantasies about their writing became maladaptive, further precipitating their addiction to drugs, alcohol, and, in Sexton's case, suicidal ideation. In the earliest stages of their alcohol and drug use, King and Sexton both fantasized that substances would be the omnipotent solution for the problems they encountered in life. For these writers, drugs were magical potions that could save them – healing their narcissistic wounds, protecting them from the harsh realities of their lives, and making their dreams come true.

The increasingly insatiable needs for narcissistic illusions to be gratified through creative output and substances became self-fulfilling prophecies. In other words, the desperation of their need to succeed in life may have pushed them further toward failure in resorting to self-destructive behaviors. Experiencing the success they so craved, they feared failure even more. In their desperation to blunt anxieties tied to the looming prospect of failure, their substance abuse problems continued to escalate. King and Sexton both initially declared that their substance use promoted their creative energies. Sometimes they gave a tremendous amount of credit to drugs and alcohol for making an acclaimed book or poem possible. And yet the more praise they received, the higher the stakes became. With the stakes raised, they found their drinking and drug use incurring more costs than benefits, further increasing the risk of the very fall from grace they feared most.

King and Sexton's fantasies about their own social identities and gender roles were often entwined in their substance abuse. King spoke of the "Hemingway defense" that had become so ingrained in his psychological framework – he was convinced that drinking was the only way that a "real" man might function under the weight of the human condition. King loathed exposing his friends and family to the fears he experienced throughout life. He drank beer, smoked cigarettes, and used drugs to keep himself buttoned up. As with his writing, substance abuse offered King omnipotent control over his fears.

On the other hand, Sexton grew up with parents who treated alcohol as a staple of the everyday life of socialites. The martini glass was a status symbol for Sexton. Sexton's substance abuse supported her narcissistic illusions about her place in the world as a woman. Perhaps linked to her fantasies about transforming the traditional role of women in society, she flaunted her self-proclaimed identity as a "drunk." She proudly wore her substance abuse on her sleeve and defied society's expectations for a woman to be polite and reserved. Furthermore, as one of the first women to publicly discuss taboo subjects, such as mental illness, sexuality, abortion, and addiction, perhaps Sexton believed on some level that alcohol could provide her with the courage she needed to stand in front of the very "proper" audiences at poetry readings and unapologetically deliver her unsettling truths.

Whereas there are many similarities in the omnipotent fantasies fueling King's and Sexton's relationships with alcohol and drugs, there are striking differences in their ultimate resolution. After many years, King finally achieved sobriety through his involvement in 12-step programs, and he remains sober after 20 years. Although he has periodically compared his writing to therapy, King has remained averse to psychotherapy:

> I'd be afraid that it would put a hole in the bottom of my bucket, and then everything might go out the wrong way ... I don't know if it would exactly destroy me as a writer, but I think it would take away a lot of the good stuff.
>
> (Rogak, 2008, p. 160)

In stark contrast to King, Sexton viewed therapy as the very source of her creativity. She often described her psychoanalytic treatment as the portal through which unconscious conflicts blossomed into striking and emotionally evocative poetry. Sexton's obsession and addictive impulses toward suicide also differed from King's ability to recover, as she experienced extreme highs and lows of psychological suffering. In contrast, King often suffered a vague, nagging sense of unhappiness, which he attributed to existential anxieties, but he encountered his deepest depression when attempting to get sober. Nonetheless, the psychological manifestations of King's struggles appear to have been less debilitating than Sexton's, since she ultimately killed herself.

Having the support of his wife and children as well as his beneficial external and internal mother figure, King was better positioned to recover. He seemed more willing to accept the help of loved ones, while holding fast to the healthy idea of his own strength and resiliency. Though married and a mother, Sexton had ambivalent attachments and felt terribly alone, an embodied perspective established in childhood that continued throughout her life.

In summary, King and Sexton inhabited an "enchanted forest" of narcissistic illusions and omnipotent fantasies, both healthy and maladaptive. Although narcissistic illusion fed their capacity to transform their experiences of self, others, and the world through creative production, they also found themselves plagued by omnipotent fantasies attached to bad internal objects and substance abuse. Both knew that their incessant angst held grave danger; Sexton called hers a "gnawing, pestilent rat" (1975/1999j) and King (2000) described his as a switch in his head he couldn't turn off. Both answered their painful yearnings through creative writing and substance abuse. When their addictions and writing careers had simultaneously reached their peaks, Sexton and King seemed willing to die chasing their omnipotent fantasies. King found his way out of the bind; Sexton did not.

Theories of narcissistic illusion dichotomize mental life into classifications of either creative and adaptive or constricting and defensive. Many of the theories we have considered portray creativity as a generally adaptive capacity nourished by narcissistic illusions stemming from "good enough" developmental processes and healthy modes of organizing self (Kohut, 1971/2011; Mitchell, 1988; Novick & Novick, 2001, 2003; Winnicott, 1971). But is reality that cut and dry?

We think not. That creative behaviors simply emerge from healthy, adaptive illusion is an overly simplistic idea, and some theorists challenge that notion (Fromm, 1956; Klein, 1929; Knafo, 2012; Rank, 1932/1989; Seinfeld, 1991; Wurmser, 2000). Creative production also issues from the traumatic damage of abuse and neglect. Illusions born in this darkness attempt adaptation but may not be healthy. Yet they can support the creation of great art. In his brilliant self-portraits, Egon Schiele captured, articulated, and transcended traumatic damage and realized greatness. Other artists symbolically create what was missing in early life (Knafo, 2012). Oppressed by childhoods rife with abuse and neglect, many artists use their creativity to address personal and existential issues.

For these artists, the work itself may become addictive, its energy imbued with demons not angels. They run to the computer or the canvas the way the alcoholic runs to the bottle. Both come away soused, the former with vision, the latter with alcohol, but the artist has something to show for it. Yet this kind of artist suffers when first inspired, while producing, when completing a work, and even when receiving recognition. As one such artist friend confided to Knafo, "I've got two choices. Either I write, or I drive the bus off the cliff. Whether it's good or bad is almost beside the point. The point is to stay alive. Good is secondary. Publishing is the least of my worries." Isolation, compulsion, fear of the page, canvas, or unformed stone, the search for repair, the gesture of transcendence, the suffering that demands action – this is what the artist faces alone, armed only with a pen or a brush or a chisel – and of course the narcissistic conviction that somehow the battle can be won.

From this viewpoint, narcissistic illusions are not always healthy, and not so different from those accompanying compulsive drug use, especially when structured from early trauma. Illusion can be healthy in some respects and unhealthy in others, now pointing the way to heaven, now hell. We might think of omnipotent fantasy as a universal human force that supports the desire to survive and thrive. The force gives rise to "illusions" – partially known ideas, images, dreams, self-concepts – that serve as a motivational template for action in the world.

Chapter 6

The sorcerer stoned

Quentin's case

The universe is full of magic things patiently waiting for our wits to grow sharper.

Phillpotts (1918)

This chapter looks at a clinical case to show how one patient's omnipotent fantasies fueled both his creativity and drug use; he used the "magic" of drugs to deaden extreme psychological pain. The therapist (Kahoud), came to the conclusion at the end of a difficult year that he and Quentin could work together to help him cast out the destructive imagos of his parents and repair his relationship with himself.

Quentin looked vacant when I first met him, as if the life had been sucked out of him with a straw, leaving behind the empty man in the waiting room. Thirty, white, and single, he worked as an English professor at a local college by day and he was a self-professed "fiction writer with limited success" by night. He was also a connoisseur of the anti-anxiety drug Xanax. Reluctant to talk at first, Quentin admitted his attorney had referred him to me after he was arrested for criminal possession of a controlled substance – namely, Xanax. He'd been mandated by the court to attend three psychotherapy sessions each week for a minimum of one year. He dragged himself from the waiting room and dumped his body onto the couch across from me. Even his flat, monotone voice sounded dead.

And yet, while the tone of his voice lacked affect, his words were heavy with omnipotence. When I first asked him what brought him to my office, he came alive, blasting his fantasies at me in short bursts from beneath the surface of his defenses, like Zeus throwing lightning bolts. He claimed to be strong and capable, only needing a bit of tweaking. He could read me by the arrangement of my office and the artwork on the walls. I was good at what I did, he instantly deduced. I'd have him back on his feet in no time. This might even be easy and fun. Psychotherapy would be the "magic bullet" that would finally break that last barrier, the one that kept constricting his potential and preventing his "success," and I would be the magician who "fixed" him.

"I'd like to hear about what part of you is broken." I said.

Quentin explained he was addicted to Xanax, since he had an "extremely addictive personality" and "bad anxiety." He described a need to "always feel good and in control." So while appearing deadened on the surface, in his fantasies Quentin was much more than merely alive. Somewhere in the back of his mind, he felt he could not accept the constraints of life as a mere mortal. He'd lived out the week before his arrest in terror because he had no more Xanax and was going through very painful and anxiety-producing withdrawal. His drug dealer told him that Xanax was in high demand – and short supply – and another week might pass before the next batch arrived. "But I didn't *have* a week," Quentin exclaimed, emotion finally coming into his voice. "I couldn't function with the anxiety – I felt like I would die without my Xanax."

He grew increasingly frantic waiting to hear from his drug dealer. On the night of his arrest, he received the all-important message just after getting into bed. Quentin popped up faster than a kid on Christmas morning. Santa Claus had come to town! Relief flooded his body, and he felt as if he could "fly around the room," and then run to meet the dealer "faster than the Flash," a comic book superhero capable of lightning speed. Minutes after showing up to meet his "doctor" in a Starbucks parking lot, Quentin realized he'd been set up. Upon exiting his dealer's car with a bag of 100 Xanax pills stuffed into the back pocket of his jeans, he found himself being handcuffed by two police officers. After being taken into custody, Quentin felt "trapped" inside the confines of his jail cell, and more than ever before, he was "utterly helpless to take control over the situation."

Quentin's words revealed a stark contrast between feelings of powerlessness and depression and omnipotent fantasies – the yearnings to overcome his powerlessness – that struck me again and again as he recounted the week of his arrest and fantasies of repairing himself to move forward into the future. He repeated certain phrases:

- *trapped potential*
- *amazing energy*
- *becoming a success*
- *breaking through walls*
- *very limited success*
- *constricting my potential*
- *fix me*
- *helpless to take control*
- *the constraints of life*
- *a mere human, flawed.*

I asked myself why Quentin found himself hurled into these chasms of depression, obsessive fantasies, and tormenting compulsions. Where did this begin and why had it found a home in his mind? What would happen when

Quentin didn't get what he wanted from me? Would he storm off like a disgruntled child? Would that plunge him even deeper into his addiction? Would he need what he wanted from the treatment *now?* Could he wait and tolerate the ambiguity of therapy with its unknown outcome? How would his addiction play out in therapy? And did he really believe he needed help, or was he playing along for legal reasons?

Quentin's stunted childhood and adolescence

During our second session, we began to explore Quentin's childhood. He recalled that as a boy he had been "obsessed" with superheroes. He spent hours dressing up as Superman and disguising himself as Clark Kent, only to reveal the omnipotent being beneath the jacket, tie, and black-rimmed glasses. Quentin described how, between the ages of four and six, he loved re-enacting the transformation from Clark Kent to Superman.

"Sounds like you had a lot of fantasies of becoming more powerful – immortal even," I said.

Quentin agreed. "I still do," he said. "That's part of how I ended up here." As a child he also placed great value on the relationships he had, through the secret conduit of his mother, with magical fantasy characters such as Santa Claus and the Easter Bunny. Quentin's tone changed after bringing his mother into the picture. He became rather cynical then, very concrete and preoccupied with "reality," calling his mother "delusional" for investing so much energy in "her make-believe bullshit." He believed that his mother had done this so her children would never grow up. He further explained that his mother was very avoidant of the topic of sex. She refused to answer any questions he had about sex as he was growing up and would walk out of the room whenever there was kissing or material even remotely sexual on television.

"So how did your mom deal with your growing up and becoming independent?"

"She didn't," he answered summarily. I asked Quentin how he was able to break free from his mother's "magic fortress" and start accepting some of the realities of life. "What was it like when you began to encounter other kids whose faith in these magical entities clashed with your own?" I asked.

Quentin said entering adolescence was "jumping from a crib into a seat behind the wheel of a car." His mother held steadfast to the worldview she created for her "little boy," both explicitly and implicitly. When he questioned her about magical beliefs, Quentin found her frighteningly dogmatic. For instance, until Quentin was 12, he was taunted by classmates for his delusional belief in Santa Claus, elves, angels, spirit guides, and other nonmaterial beings. Nonetheless, Mom maintained these figures *were* real, and urged him not to listen to his friends whom Santa no longer visited. She became anxious and retreated if Quentin attempted to discuss sex. And even when Quentin began to notice he needed deodorant, his mother was unwilling to help him out, asserting that he was "too young." Quentin's mother was terrified to let her "little boy" go – and perhaps even more so, she could not let go of the magic that helped her to obscure her own intolerable realities. As Quentin matured physically, the walls of his mother's house were her magical palace, but for him they were a prison that confined his psychological growth.

On the other hand, Quentin told me that his mother was a creative writer, instilling in him a love of literature and writing. During his childhood, she introduced him to imaginative literature and nurtured his own creative urges. Quentin grew up to be an avid reader and fiction writer, which put him on the path to becoming an English professor. Because he had been able to use the magic of his childhood to foster these academic career pursuits as an adult, he remained connected to the coveted fantasy world of his childhood.

As Quentin's writing became the primary outlet for his creativity, his mother reacted effusively to everything he wrote – for a while. As he got older and entered high school, his writing changed. If a story became too "real" for his mother – meaning it contained sex, violence, or other "adult content" she deemed "inappropriate" – it was either passively ignored, disapproved of, or shown a form of appreciation that felt blatantly fraudulent.

While his mother would not tolerate anything less than merger with Quentin to fulfill her psychological needs, his father was quite the opposite – a distant, brooding alcoholic whose primary mode of relating to his son was through aggression. Although he rarely punished his son with beatings, Quentin described the intensity of his father's anger as terrifying.

> He was a screamer. I mean, a fucking screamer. His eyes would pop out like the eyes of those wacky cartoon characters, and it was anything but funny. And the tendons of his neck would stand out like cables stretched to breaking. And he'd be screaming so loud, spit flying out of his mouth, bursting blood vessels in his eyes, I'd think they could hear him screaming two states over. It scared the crap out of me.

Quentin often recalled being screamed at by his father for being "disrespectful" or getting in trouble at school. His father intimidated him physically by chasing after him and threatening violence, although he rarely followed through on those threats. Quentin vividly recalled crouching on the floor in whatever corner of the house he found himself backed into, the pungent stench of alcohol still lingering in the air from his father's presence. Quentin curled up in a ball, either sobbing or staring off into space, retreating inward while the echoes of his father's rage continued to rain down upon him. Immediately following such punishments, Quentin's father would storm out of the house, slamming the door behind him, sometimes not returning for days.

Although Quentin's mother was passive and his father aggressive, both parents defended themselves through avoidance. Over the course of Quentin's life, his father had been repeatedly arrested for drunk driving and spent more than a few nights in jail. Eventually, his parents separated. Quentin was 15 when they were officially divorced, and his mother received full custody due to his father's arrests for driving while intoxicated. Following his parents' divorce, Quentin rarely saw his father, but he remembered his encounters with the man in vivid detail. Whatever pieces were missing from his image of his father were filled in by his mother, and she spared him none of the painful details. Quentin's father spent most of his time at bars, and at one point he had had an ongoing affair with a woman he met at the local tavern. Quentin described memories of his mother "walking on eggshells" around her "angry alcoholic" husband at the time they separated.

Quentin watched his mother become increasingly depressed, nervous, fragile, and socially withdrawn during his high school years. He remembered how, if he came home from school feeling happy or excited, he'd feel guilty upon seeing his sad mother. She was "too miserable to be happy for her son," he told me. When he felt good, her responses to him generally felt forced, fake, and inconsistent. Yet, if Quentin became sad or upset, she gave him the love and attention he craved. Only then did he feel she displayed genuine care and compassion. Perhaps most troubling was his mother's inability to tolerate his anger. Whenever he expressed frustration with his mother to any degree, she retreated to her bedroom and hid behind a closed door. If he "got into trouble at school," she threatened to call his father and have him come over to "punish" him. As he recounted this interaction to me, Quentin wondered aloud, "Why didn't she just punish me herself?"

Searching for magic

Quentin became insecure and socially anxious after he left home for college. Rather than discovering new relationships in friends or romantic interests away from home, he retreated to a childhood fantasy world in which he played the hero in every imagined scenario. He experienced difficulties establishing relationships in college due to his social anxiety. Soon he entered into a relationship that would become one of his greatest loves and most painful losses – the one he cultivated with mind-altering chemicals.

Early in the treatment, Quentin talked about his history of substance abuse and the way different chemicals made him feel. He had always been a drinker and smoked marijuana on and off since high school, depicting himself as being mentally bound up by his anxiety for as long as he could remember. He believed that he could not function socially without being drunk or high. Quentin stated that alcohol occasionally got him into trouble in high school, leading him to commit random acts of foolishness such as urinating in public, directly beside the parked police car he failed to notice. And marijuana often made him feel "dumb as a brick," stuck so far inside his own head that he was unable to find his way out for the chance to connect with others. Still, the side effects of booze and marijuana were well worth their cost, since inebriation brought temporary peace to an inner world riddled with anxiety, insecurity, and self-loathing. Substances brought relief to a long-lived pain that he didn't realize existed until he was free from it. Quentin encountered cocaine and ecstasy during his freshman year of college, but quickly found stimulants did not contain the magic he so desperately needed. While the moments of euphoria with cocaine and ecstasy made him feel omnipotent for a brief time, they both led to rapid "comedowns" in which anxiety rained down harder than ever. Quentin learned all about the "rebound effect," and by sophomore year he had moved on from the stimulants that so predictably worsened his anxious disposition.

It was toward the end of his college career that Quentin met his true love, the only "one" that had the power to release him from the prison of his own mind. All it took was a quick "pop" of the tiny oval. Benzodiazepines increase the availability of neurotransmitters that inhibit anxiety and quiet the harsh and judgmental voice of the superego. When Quentin first began experimenting with Xanax, he found that he was *set free* from the mind that had been holding him hostage for so long. Finally experiencing freedom from the prison of an anguished psyche, he became utterly dependent after just one night with that lovely white pill. "It went 'pop' and relief ... wake up and repeat as needed," he remarked. "And it was almost always needed."

I asked Quentin to tell me more about how Xanax changed the way he felt about himself.

"Well ... I think I've always felt like there is something wrong with me," he said.

> Like I have some serious defect or something. And I was so lonely. It seemed the more people I was around, the more alone I felt. The loneliness was overwhelming. And not only that, but I would get angry about feeling so alone. Angry at my helplessness. So, I was mean. I was never the "jolly drunk." I was self-destructive. And I scared my friends away, ruining relationships and giving up any chance I had of finding new ones.
>
> But who needed people? The drugs became friends that I could keep with me in my pocket all night. They would go into my body and become a part of my mind. I became "one" with them. And then no one else mattered. 'Fuck 'em,' I would think to myself. Once I had enough drugs, I could go back to my room and be alone without difficulty, high and happy enough. It was all good ... until the high wore off. No problem, take more drugs. Drugs run out? No problem, get more. The trouble starts when I can't get a new order before I'm out. Then, it's like all the horrible shit the drugs keep at bay comes crashing through the door like a swat team and beats me to a bloody pulp. Guilt, hating myself, bone-chilling loneliness. Without the drugs, all I have is the abyss.

The aftermath

Despite a rapid progression in the use of addictive substances, Quentin was able to function well enough in college. His grades were decent, and he even had time to write on weekends. The progression of his drug abuse seemed typical, but the way he coped with the aftermath of the weekends of heavy drug use once Monday arrived was not typical. Consumed by depression and anxiety, he spent much of his weekday mornings and afternoons – either after class or instead of class – holed up and isolated in a library cubicle. It was the only place he felt safe. No one could find him if he found the right location, usually a nook hidden in a far-off, deserted corner of the second or third floor of the library. There he would write in solitude. With his laptop plugged into the outlet beneath him, Quentin would punch away at the keyboard for hours, writing fiction.

As he later realized, everything he wrote was about himself, fueled by the residues of guilt and shame he experienced while thinking back on his behavior over the weekend. When I asked for memories of his fantasies while writing, Quentin recalled:

> I remember imagining my stories would connect me to people who would want more and more of me. I remember the fantasies that my writing would *make* others love and want me. I wouldn't have to say or do anything in person. If they just read my work, they would love me. And that was all I needed. To feel loved.

Sometimes, Quentin reported, the walls of his depression felt too thick to break through, and he found he couldn't write at all. His creativity was blunted and his mind became dull and thoughtless. Still, the isolation of the cubicle provided him with a sense of solace from what he perceived to be a harsh and punitive external world. The three walls extending up and around the sides of the desk were like protective barriers – real and symbolic – against his fear and anguish about what his life was becoming. His description of the cubicle invited comparisons with the containing function of the therapy room – a safe place where he could have his pain held, contained, reflected back, and articulated in meaningful words.

By the end of his senior year of college, Quentin completed his first work of fiction. It took place in the future, a time when pharmaceutical drug technology was far advanced beyond that of the crude antidepressants, stimulants, and tranquilizers used to treat mental health disorders today. In the story, a young man named Louis had spent his life on an endless search for something to correct a fundamental sense of being flawed. He felt a deep void inside, a deprivation of some relentless need. Like Quentin, Louis found no relief until he encountered drugs. In the quest to drown out the pain of his emptiness, Louis became addicted to drugs. After a concerned friend recommended a doctor for Louis's addiction, he was prescribed a trial of an experimental new medication called Reversol. The once-daily pill was known to cure all addictive behaviors and promised to safely rewire the circuitry in regions of the brain responsible for cravings, impulse control, consequential thinking, emotion management, and compulsive behaviors. Louis enjoyed his newfound sobriety but only for a short while. Soon he began to dig himself back down into his old ditch. After applying and being hired for a menial custodial position in the lab where this medication was produced, Louis began stealing and selling the pills to drug addicts on the streets of Manhattan.

In essence, Louis's sober state became just as addictive as a drug, and he found himself increasingly obsessed with the way it had "magically transformed" his life. It is then that his doctor told him that Reversol was actually a placebo. Shocked at the power of placebo and impressed with the strength of his own mind free from all chemicals, Louis decided to find a therapist and begin psychotherapy.

Through his fiction, Quentin expressed that addiction is far more complex than just shutting off reward pathways in the brain. By the story's end, Louis discovered he was using concrete "things" to fill the void of those experiences he felt deprived of – perhaps the unmet needs from his childhood, which he could not remember. Although Quentin showed insight into the addictive behavior of his fictional Louis, his own self-knowledge seemed superficial. He stayed mostly on the surface in our dialogue, repeating a narrative that was in sharp contrast to the complexity of the struggles of the character in his story.

Dueling dragons

As the treatment progressed, I began considering two distinct modes in which Quentin and I were relating to each other. In the treatment room, Quentin seemed to walk on eggshells around me. I found him ingratiating, unnecessarily apologetic, exaggeratedly thoughtful, and obsequious about how he was doing in analysis. Nine months into the first year of the analysis, I found myself regularly irritated with Quentin. The irritation turned to anger, and before long, I found myself sitting with sadistic fantasies of punching Quentin in the face. Those reveries became disturbing.

In my own analysis, I found myself preoccupied with feelings of anger toward Quentin. I spoke of my fantasies of verbally abusing him, telling him to *shut the fuck up* as he apologized for his part in my abusiveness. My analyst pointed out that she had never heard such hatred in my voice. Nor had I. When I thought of Quentin, I felt aggressive and controlling. I felt the force of anger rising up from within, surfacing at a frightening pace. In sadistic omnipotent fantasies that I later uncovered, seeing them in retrospect as they hovered hidden beneath the surface of my conscious awareness, I had made Quentin my captive. He would answer only to me. I would make empty promises to provide Quentin with the relief he was seeking, to fill the void, and extinguish the deprivation he experienced in his cavernous need to squelch his desire – tantalizing him and then withdrawing the panacea – an omnipotent, healing solution. In these fantasies, I began to embody the drugs he was dependent on, creating a dialectical bond between myself as his omnipotent, sadistic self and Quentin's insatiable neediness, obsessiveness, and power-lessness. And then I had fantasies of rejecting and failing him, ending the treatment, leaving him alone and in tremendous pain.

I was certain that Quentin's dissociated rage had put a spell on my uncon-scious, but I soon began to see my own unconscious rage through my identi-fication with Quentin's depressive self. Like Quentin, I realized that in my own personal relationships I too was cut off from my anger, terrified of my own rage. And like Quentin, it often manifested for me in a chronic, fatiguing depressive state – a state my own mother displayed and my own father appeared cut off from. Bearing some resemblance to Quentin's parents, my own mother played the martyr, and my father was overly aggressive. Although neither parent expressed the extremes of Quentin's, still the simi-larity was enough to trigger my disturbing countertransference.

Informed by my countertransference fantasies, I explored Quentin's experi-ence of himself. He described strong, conflicting identifications with both mother and father. For Quentin, it was the identification with his mother that was the more conscious mode in which he experienced himself. The "good" mother he had internalized was innocent, kind, and creative; the "bad" mother was depressed, hopeless, and weak. Much less conscious and barely within reach of his awareness was the identification with his father, which he had internalized and blocked off from the maternal imago from an early age.

Regardless of which caregiver he was identified with, the emotional void he felt inside never changed. When identified with his mother, he worked to fill that hole with his creativity – spinning fantasies of becoming a successful writer, pleasing his mother, and acquiring friends and legions of fans. He imagined that this love – the love of his mother, his friends, and the fans of his future novels – would fill the emptiness he experienced. When identified with his mother, he isolated himself, and the fantasies were sublimated into either creative pursuits, such as writing, or a depression that left him bedridden but served as a defense against the aggressive, omnipotent identification with his father.

Furthermore, identification with his mother interfered with his developing healthy relationships with women since sex for her had been such a problem. She'd been disgusted, perhaps even terrified, by sexual relations and had effectively communicated that to her son. Quentin subsequently became awkward, shy, and inept in the bedroom. His sexual self-consciousness and sexual guilt made him afraid of women and further isolated him from the intimacy he desperately desired. It took some time for us the address this issue since it was the source of much of his pain, and we both needed to get past some of the negative transferences that had developed in therapy and cultivate a deeper sense of trust in each other.

When identified with his father, Quentin had little capacity to reflect on himself, identify his emotions, or manage his impulses. He was a "tough guy," a "strong, powerful man." In reality, he conceived of finding his strength in the substances. Quentin's omnipotent solutions and fantasies of self-transformation depended on mind-altering drugs. They defended against the vulnerabilities, helplessness, and powerlessness he experienced. Like his father, Quentin was cut off from these feelings. Whether identified with his mother or his father, Quentin lacked awareness of the incompatible parts of his personality – they disappeared into unconscious fantasies. Not surprisingly, when Quentin was arrested, he recalled sitting in the jail cell overnight, repeatedly thinking to himself, "How did this happen? This is not *me*! *I* am not a criminal! *I* am not a bad person! How could this be possible?"

The sorcerer stoned

Quentin often put his head down and looked at the floor when discussing his experience of "hitting bottom" – especially when relating to his substance abuse. But one time he looked up at me after describing an experience that was especially shameful for him and said:

> I still remember, just after getting myself arrested, I was aware on some level that I felt like giving up. I just didn't care anymore. But something kept driving me to make it all go away. Or maybe it was *me* I was looking to escape from. Either way, I was aware that I was becoming obsessed with the pills, and in denial about where I knew I was heading if I kept heading down that road.

I asked Quentin if he would say more about the "power of these substances," and he described the way pills could almost instantaneously transform him:

> I could be the person I wanted to be. It felt like I could actually be *me*. Not some extreme caricature of one of my parents or the other. I was no longer locked away behind this lost, frightened, sad version of myself. And when I wasn't able to achieve the kind of high that made me feel invincible, drugs at least gave me the power to just not care if I was me or not.

"And then?" I asked.

> Well, when I started to go through withdrawal, after I'd been on these things for long periods of time, I became extremely desperate to get more. I would run around like a maniac to track down my dealer. I was absolutely terrified of what it felt like to be in withdrawal. You can't even imagine how fucking scary it is to be out of dope when you start getting

sick. Once I finally got a hold of a few Percocets; it was like I waved a magic wand and became normal again.

I asked Quentin to describe the powers of that "magic wand."

"It just made things better. It made me okay. I finally was able to get some relief." I wondered with Quentin about what he might be seeking relief from. "Before I found Xanax, I was never able to feel good. I never felt even okay. I felt ashamed of who I was. Like there was something wrong with the real me, and nothing I did would ever get rid of that shame."

I nodded in understanding, and we sat for a few moments of silence before I offered an interpretation:

> So you would hide from yourself when you were high on drugs like your mother hid from you ... and when the "withdrawals" showed up, you ended up running in fear, as if you were being chased down and cornered by your father. There are these two separate parts of you participating in the drug use. And they are extreme selves. The extremes your mother and father symbolically represent in you. There is no grey area. No middle ground. And these separate parts of you that you took from your parents have been at war all your life. I think it is time you call a truce.

A recurring dream

As Quentin was coming close to completing his one year of mandated treatment, he stated that he might want to continue therapy after his sentencing. Perhaps identifying with me, he was also thinking about going to graduate school to become a psychotherapist. It was around this time that Quentin first brought in a recurring dream he remembered having during childhood. He stopped having the dream around the time he entered middle school, but remembered his mother saying he first told her about it as early as five or six years old.

"I'm sitting at the table with my mother and aunt (her sister), waiting to eat dinner," Quentin began.

> I know we are waiting for my father to join us at the table, but he isn't around during this part of the dream. I am also aware that my mother and her sister are whispering to each other, taking extra measures to exclude me from the conversation by covering their mouths with their hands. Then they begin to giggle and turn to me. My mother asks me to join them in playing a "funny joke" on my father when he arrives. She asks me to wait until my father sits down and then reach over and tug at his ears. I remember feeling special that my mother and aunt were including me in planning their game. I felt eager to earn their love and respect, but I also felt hesitant to pull my father's ears.

So my father arrives and sits next to me, and the pressure to comply builds up. I reach out and grab onto my father's ears, pulling on them. Initially, I am startled by the laughter of my mother and aunt across the table from my father and me. But then I see why they are taunting my father, and I am horrified. The act of pulling on his ears makes something terrible happen to him … triggers a kind of … mechanism that releases a thick, dark liquid which begins pouring out of his ears, splashing down over his shoulders and onto his face and neck. My father turns to me, red in the face, as the liquid continues to rush from the two sides of his face. He is humiliated, and my betrayal enrages him. The laughter continues to fill the room as my father's face grows redder and more furious, and I feel panic while I'm waiting for him to explode. All at once, I feel my mother has betrayed me. I feel ashamed of what I've done to my father. And I feel terror over what is about to happen – and then it ends. While I didn't know what alcohol or liquor smelled like at that age, I recognized the pungent odor of the liquid flowing from his ears as an odor that my father emitted constantly. Later in life, I came to identify the smell, the odor that was so overpowering in the dream, as whiskey.

This dream encapsulates and symbolizes Quentin's plight, established at a young age. His mother encouraged passivity and helplessness. She loved him when he felt and displayed pain. Pain became the indicator of his worth, the currency earning him her acceptance. Only when disabled could he receive her love. Although she encouraged his fantasy life and creativity, she discouraged his meetings with reality. She mirrored brokenness, and in her Quentin saw himself broken. She castrated him slowly and gently, refusing any display of his aggression. She removed herself and her love whenever he began to fight his sense of loss and weakness. She refused to be present to any change. She signaled to him that his sexual desire was wrong, his need to face reality bad, his manhood problematic. Note the masturbatory symbolism in the dream, the tugging on the father's ears, which releases a putrid and humiliating climax, devastating and enraging the father who is then turned against the son. Note, too, the collusion between the mother and her sister, excluding Quentin at first and then taking him in as a dupe. These images are remarkably condensed: masturbation, Oedipal guilt, betrayal and killing, the mystery of the female, murderous rage seething beneath the facade of family, the anguished longing for love.

His father also wreaked destruction on Quentin's self-esteem and sense of self. He is not initially present in the dream, just as he was not there for his son. He did nothing to support his son's budding manhood. Just the opposite, he attacked it repeatedly. He screamed Quentin out of existence and then abandoned him, showing him neither love nor pride. His violent abuse and cold neglect expressed his own helplessness, for he was an addict who hated himself and transferred that hatred onto his son. He taught his son how to hate himself.

The triangle is complex. The mother, though passive and fearful, kept secrets with herself, secrets that she unconsciously communicated to her son. At an early age, Quentin already knew this unconsciously, and furthermore, he even knew what those secrets were. *Your father is more helpless than I am. He's a loser, little more than a furious container of booze. He's a thing, a mechanism, a jug whose handles, should you tug them, reveal his essence, a stinking brown liquid. Shit, booze, polluted and diseased blood. That's your father. He is no good. And you, unless you become sexless, passive, and accepting of futility, will become like him.* The father probably knew (unconsciously) that the mother used the son in her conflict with him. Perhaps when he screamed at his son, he was screaming at the mother. He may have feared his own violence, and that was why he would leave the house after an outburst. Or it may also be he wasn't merely walking out on the son. Thus, Quentin became the container for the resentment, hatred, and violence his parents directed toward each other. They psychologically tore him in two.

Both parents were helpless: the father against his addiction, the mother against her deadness. They all but killed their son's vitality, they sapped his spirit, they imprisoned him in a lonely cubicle in which his thoughts could not be suffered, understood, or accepted. The best he could do was to crush them with drugs or leak them out in his writing. And he could not write beyond the limits of his repetitive, deadening pain. He was so buried in his parents' deadness that his fiction did not offer him any real possibilities of psychological liberation. Only Xanax dulled the agony. This is the "bottom" he finally hit when he sought help.

As Quentin recounted the dream, I could clearly hear the conflict between his internalized mother and father, pushing and pulling him in opposing directions, tearing his sense of self into shreds. But unlike the themes that Quentin consciously spoke about in therapy, the dream revealed the aspects of his unconscious left unarticulated. Beneath the surface, his mother was not just passive and submissive. She was not just the victim of an angry alcoholic husband. She too had aggression and rage – no matter how deeply buried it might be. And his father was not only the aggressor – not just the abusive miser he became in Quentin's mind. His mother and father were just as vulnerable as any other human being. They each had different ways of shielding themselves from the pain of those vulnerabilities, variegated and complex methods of defense that developed to handle the wreckage of their own unmet needs. And they each were human – just as human as Quentin would begin to feel someday. I think I may have heard the first glimpses of that belief in his voice as he recalled the recurring dream for the first time in my office. That was also the first time I strongly felt we would do some very good work together.

Conclusion

Omnipotent fantasies for a disenchanted world

> A healthy relationship with one's fantasy life is reflected by a subtle, dialectical balance between illusions and reality, wherein illusions are continuously generated, playfully enjoyed, and relinquished in the face of disappointments.
>
> Stephen A. Mitchell (1988)

This volume has examined ways that omnipotent fantasies are used to develop psychological conditions from which both creativity and addiction emerge. We have considered the similarities and differences between the magical illusions driving creativity and those at the root of compulsive sex and drug use. In addition, we have illustrated how both maladaptive, rigid illusions can coexist alongside flexible, adaptive illusions that foster creativity, as is the case with countless creative writers, painters, musicians, actors, and other artists who have battled life-threatening addictions.

A number of the theories we reviewed neatly dichotomize mental life, with an individual's developmental history either self-preservative or self-destructive. Such theories present omnipotent fantasies as forms of mental energy that can be split off into binaries – the pure, adaptive, benevolent form of omnipotence that carries great potential for creativity, and the pathological form that leads to destructive behavior. It can be tempting to conclude that omnipotence will emerge in the direction of growth or destruction simply depending on whether a person is nourished by "good enough" developmental processes and healthy modes of organizing the self and others (Kohut, 1971; Mitchell, 1988; Winnicott, 1971). For instance, Mitchell asserted that the quality of the caregiver's illusions in relation to the child has a profound impact on how the child comes to use their own magic, invoking the myth of Icarus and Daedalus. He said it is the caregiver's participation in the child's illusions that ultimately determines "whether … [the child] can fly high enough to enjoy them [his or her narcissistic illusions] and truly soar … or whether the sense of ponderous necessity concerning the illusions leads one to fly too high or to never leave the ground" (Mitchell, 1988, p. 199).

Nonetheless, other theories challenge the notion that a "good enough" developmental experience is what inspires the magic of creativity as opposed to the omnipotence of compulsive sex and drugs (Fromm, 1956; Klein, 1929/ 2002; Rank, 1932/1989; Seinfeld, 1991; Wurmser, 2000). For example, Wurmser (1979, 2000) portrayed both healthy and maladaptive surface behaviors as reflecting narcissistic illusions that emerge in the face of conflict, suffering, and wish fulfillment. He and others asked, without the disappoint-ments and pains inherent in early development and interpersonal relation-ships, where might one find the sparks that ignite creative processes? Indeed, many creative writers and artists reflect on their work as a process that seeks to create that which was missing in early life (Knafo, 2012).

The human mind is inherently conflicted – a source of vitality and degra-dation – and navigating omnipotent fantasies is a complex process, fraught with paradoxes. We propose that the quality of a person's relationship to the fantasies themselves is what determines how omnipotence takes shape and finds expression in variegated behaviors. As such, fantasy life is set to the tune of one's capacity for balancing the magic of illusions with the reason of rea-lity. This concept has parallels to conceptualizations dating back to philoso-phers of the nineteenth century. For instance, Nietzsche (1872/1956) described the tragic struggle of humankind to achieve a mental state of harmony by balancing illusions and reality. The philosopher thought the most desirable internal experiences were rooted in a delicate balance among creative, artistic, and symbolic aspects of mental life rather than rigid views of reality. For Nietzsche, new illusions can be continually created and dissolved if one relates to them with flexibility. Omnipotent fantasies can serve adaptive functions if a person retains the capacity to let go of them when the harsh winds of reality overshadow such illusions and/or when they no longer promote growth.

Sex, drugs, and fairy tales

We will end with a creative illustration of our own theory by retelling the classic tale *Jack and the Beanstalk*. A number of versions of the English fairy tale have been told over the past century, and in every one Jack is faced with the looming threat of starvation due to severe financial strain. In every adaptation, Jack encounters a number of conflicts and dilemmas that involve complex responses to imminent annihilation. The story encompasses rescue fantasies, interpersonal conflicts, sexual desires, and a hunger for mastery in a perilous, chaotic world. The magic of omnipotence rescues Jack in difficult situations, regardless of whether the roots reach down into "good enough" soil or, alternatively, a barren wasteland.

Jack is seeking a magical solution because desperate times call for despe-rate measures – or, more appropriately for our purposes, *omnipotent* measures. Jack and his mother live alone and are in dire straits. Jack's father was the family's sole breadwinner. We do not know how his father perished, but Jack (still just an adolescent) immediately assumes the responsibilities of his late father (and, less explicitly, becomes partner to his widowed mother). Jack's mother's demands prove to be too heavy a burden to bear, often leaving her son feeling impotent and inadequate. All the pressure falls on him to save his mother (and himself). Understandably, Jack feels lost, inferior, and utterly helpless.

In one final attempt at salvation, Jack's mother sends him to town to sell their prized family cow. This is where Jack encounters a mysterious trades-man who offers him a handful of magic beans in exchange for his cow. Jack agrees to the trade – a decision that we might see as naïve, if not downright foolish. Nevertheless, it is Jack's faith in magic and a flexibility of mind in the face of danger that allows him to bend the limits of rational thought and overlook traditional wisdom. At times, his omnipotent fantasies help him crash through the boundaries of constricting realities, going beyond the limits of basic, frightening truths. There is no moment more critical for accessing the mind's magical solutions than when staring down the barrel of a gun – the drive to survive.

Some might call Jack a dreamer. And they would not be wrong. In the tale, the trader enlists Jack's narcissistic illusions to facilitate sealing the deal. He tells Jack that he senses, just from their brief conversation, that Jack is no ordinary boy. Rather, Jack is special, possessing a unique way of seeing past the surface limitations of his experience. The trader sees in Jack a boy who is not afraid to take risks, for Jack has the capacity to believe in forces that defy what is typically considered sound judgment. And, indeed, Jack sees salvation in those beans, although he doesn't necessarily know how it will come about. Thus, for our purposes, Jack's capacity for inhabiting his enchanting fantasy life – not the concrete, magic beans themselves – is what saves him and his mother and ultimately bestows great fortune upon them.

Alas, in many versions of the tale, Jack's mother deals him a harsh beating when she learns what he has traded for the precious cow, and she throws the beans out the window. But it is the anger, disappointment, and disillusion-ment of his mother that pains him most, perhaps even more than the pain of the beating. Jack's mother rigidly subscribes to the cold, hard reality that her son has been swindled. "How could you be such an idiot?" she bellows. "You've been robbed! What were you thinking? Magic beans do not exist! Now take that," repeatedly whacking Jack with the broom. "And that! And that! And as for your precious magic beans, here they go, out the window! Go fetch them in the dirt if you want to eat tonight. And don't let me see your face!"

Jack goes to bed without supper and awakens the next morning to find a massive beanstalk in his backyard, rising up from the ground where his mother tossed the magic beans the night before. The beanstalk pierces the clouds in the sky high above the tiny home where Jack and his mother live. Jack doesn't waste any time in beginning his ascent, scaling to the top, boos-ted by an intuition that his luck might change. At the top he catches sight of a castle sitting on clouds off in the distance. Jack creeps up to this big house and peers through the window. Inside, he sees a mouthwatering spread of food and a beautiful woman. He immediately calls to her, "Excuse me, Miss – I am starving. Could you spare something to eat?" The woman is gracious and kind, inviting him in. As he eats, Jack begins to notice something mysterious about the house. Some of the furniture is absurdly oversized. In fact, it almost looks like the furniture was fit for ... a giant!

Suddenly, the ground beneath Jack's feet begins to shake as the sound of pounding footsteps grows louder. The woman flies into a panic. "Quick – hide! It's my husband!" Jack runs off down the hall and tries the handle of the closest door. The door opens and Jack slips into the room, closing the door behind him and jumping under the bed. Frozen in terror, Jack hears a bellowing voice that can only be that of a giant. He hears quarrelling – and the giant's roaring suspicions that someone has been inside their home. "Fee-Fi-Fo-Fum – I smell the blood of an Englishman!" The giant's wife reassures him there is no one else in the house. "Don't be silly!" she pleads with her husband. "There is no one here but me! I've been here by myself all day waiting for your return." The giant scoffs and grumbles and goes off to his bedroom – the room where Jack is hiding under the bed.

As the giant enters the room and sits at a massive desk, Jack catches his first glimpse of an enormous pile of gold coins, some in large sacks and others stacked in shimmering rows. Jack's eyes light up, and his head begins to swell with desire. He imagines the look in his mother's eyes when he shows her the sacks of gold he has brought home to her. He sees the glory of a new life of riches. He sees flashes of bounties of food, the means to satisfy his needs and those of his mother on demand, and a glorious new home where he can someday raise a family with children of his own – the power to make things happen in his world.

As the giant counts his gold coins at the desk, Jack watches in silence with glowing, hungry eyes and a watering mouth. The counting does not last long before the giant gets sleepy and collapses on the bed just above Jack's head. Once he hears the giant snoring and is sure he has fallen asleep, Jack scrambles out from under the bed, grabs two sacks of gold coins, and runs off down the hall and out of the castle. He flies down the beanstalk and brings the money straight to his mother, who is just as delighted as his fantasies told him she would be.

Two more times Jack climbs up the beanstalk, is fed by the giant's wife, and then runs home with one of the giant's possessions while the giant's wife covers for him. Each time, the giant senses someone has been in the house, roaring his rhyme again and again: "Fee-Fi-Fo-Fum!" Each time, she swears he is wrong. While we don't know for sure, it seems as if the giant's wife is a captive rather than willing partner, and that she too is seeking her own form of salvation. Each time Jack returns, she helps him sneak in and out of the castle. On the second run, Jack presents his mother with a large golden hen that lays eggs made of solid gold.

On the third visit, Jack's omnipotence begins to put him in jeopardy for reasons that go beyond his primary need to save himself and his mother. His fantasies of a new life of great wealth and power start to become addictive. Jack wants more possessions than he needs; survival is no longer the driving force. On the third visit, he lays eyes on a magic golden harp that plays beautiful music on its own. He prepares to sneak the musical instrument out of the house, but the harp suddenly begins to cry out for its master: "Master, help me! Help me! This boy is trying to take me away!" Jack runs from the castle faster than ever, carrying the harp in his arms. In our own version, Jack takes the giant's wife with him this time, as she begs to be freed from captivity. They start their descent down the beanstalk, but soon hear the giant not far behind, his thunderous feet crashing overhead. As Jack and his new companion speedily shimmy down the beanstalk, the giant follows but is awkward and tentative as he attempts to maneuver his oversized feet over the beanstalk's branches and tortuous vines. Fortunately, Jack has an axe he has stored nearby, and when he reaches the ground, he makes haste to chop down the beanstalk. With a final blow to the shaft it tips over, and the giant loses his grip. He falls to his death as Jack and the giant's wife watch with sighs of relief. Jack goes home to his mother with the newfound love of his life and lives happily ever after.

The delicate balance

In an effort to save himself and his mother from starvation, Jack essentially uses magic to rob and kill someone, albeit a giant who is portrayed as a monstrous figure. He then marries the giant's wife and attains wealth beyond his wildest dreams. Nevertheless, Jack's salvation would not have been possible without the true magic of the beans. The magic beans are real. Thus, Jack's victory rests on a miracle – magic that defies reality and creates the impossible. Pure magic is what saves Jack from his frightening reality – if the tale is taken at face value.

For our purposes, the tale is about far more than magic in the concrete world. Rather, it is the wish, both conscious and unconscious, for magical solutions in a disenchanted world. Thus, it is Jack's capacity to believe in himself and his ability to make things happen in the concrete world that render the story meaningful to us. Our aim in invoking this fairy tale is to highlight the nuances of the magic of Jack's mind, represented in the use of omnipotent fantasies that unleash Jack's inner powers and potential for growth. When examined from this perspective, insights are revealed in the tale's symbolism that help us to flesh out our understanding of the importance of establishing a balance in people's relatedness to their omnipotence.

Through Jack's responses to his dire circumstances we see both the riches and perils to which a person may be exposed when driven by omnipotent fantasies. Also evident are the complex ways in which those outcomes relate to Jack's ability to sustain a balance between his illusions and reality. The absence of Jack's father may trigger in the boy unconscious Oedipal fantasies about replacing him and possessing his mother, as well as guilt about feeling these emotions. Jack is desperate to survive, please his mother, and make his late father proud, which is why he takes his chances on anything that might help him realize his fantasies of omnipotence.

When making the decision to trade the cow for some magic beans, Jack uses his ability to embrace his fantasies, which grant him the faith in his ability to transform his situation and the optimism that unforeseen, fortuitous circumstances might turn up as a result of taking a chance.

After climbing the beanstalk and reaching the castle in the clouds, Jack harnesses his omnipotent fantasies to swindle a giant and steal two bags of gold coins and a hen that can continually supply the needs of himself and his mother. But Jack is doing more than just robbing a giant in the external world. In fantasy, Jack is overcoming a massive inner block represented by the giant – the part of his experience that keeps him small and limited to poverty and degradation. The giant is dumbfounded by Jack's unflinching boldness, and those same omnipotent qualities allow Jack to transcend the blind, stupid parts of himself (the harsh superego of his mother and the guilt associated with living up to the potential of his deceased father), that can no longer block his path to salvation.

Again, our version of the tale adds a twist to highlight Oedipal dynamics. Returning home victorious, Jack shows his mother that the prevailing efforts of his fantasies ultimately conquer the truths of her reality. Through believing in himself and his capacity to change the world around him, Jack finally breaks away from his mother's grip and takes control of his life, allowing him the right to be married to another woman and promoted to the more powerful position of a man – to separate from his mother and break free. The magic beans and the beanstalk are symbolic of Jack's phallic conquest, an Oedipal victory that also represents magic that has the power to bridge heaven and earth. This theme is repeated in Jack's literal killing of the giant in concrete terms as well as his success in saving and possessing the giant's wife as his own.

In our interpretation of this tale, the treasures of Jack's unconscious wishes are discovered high above him in the sky. At the beginning of the story, his head is buried in the sand. By the end, he literally has his head in the clouds where the magic of his unconscious exists. The cutting down of the phallic beanstalk resulting in the giant's death can be understood as Jack's castrating the castrating power of limitation – destroying the precedent of his mother's treatment of him as a naïve child and her judgments about his "idiotic" decision to purchase the magic beans. In this sense, Jack's slaying of the giant represents his achievement of unconscious fantasies – to wrest power and reach manhood.

Like Icarus who flies too close to the sun, Jack's omnipotent fantasies threaten to get the better of him when he steals the harp (which is not needed) and must run from the giant. He loses his footing and becomes greedy, returning to a risky and dangerous situation to fulfill an addictive need for more ... and more. While traditionally this fairy tale ends in "happily ever after," we propose that a sequel to the story would reveal a great deal more. We would argue that if Jack fails to re-establish the balance between his illusions and the realities of his circumstances, the addictiveness of his relationship to his omnipotent fantasies would grow deeper and increasingly more toxic. Jack has created a situation in which he is no longer in survival mode. He has now accumulated enough wealth and is in a vulnerable position for having created an entirely new world of problems in the process of solving the original problem. Without the delicate balance that allows a person to release their grip on addictive narcissistic illusions of power, sex, and material possessions, they, like Jack, may sadly find themselves setting out for town in search of the magic bean trader, caught up in a vicious cycle driven by such addictive impulses. We now can apply Jack's adventures to real life. The beans symbolize a unique perspective of the world – an omnipotent fantasy that helps Jack break through limitations. The beans point the way toward embracing the magic of our minds and believing in ourselves and our fantasies.

Immortality and beyond

For the magic of an omnipotent fantasy to materialize in adaptive versus self-destructive behaviors requires taking some risks. The secret to the magic wand is in wielding it fearlessly but judiciously, acknowledging the limitations imposed by reality on even the best of sorcerers. The relationship one forms with fantasies involves a delicate balancing act. Perhaps poet and scientist Dale Pendell (1995, p. 10) said it best:

> An ally is not like a fairy-godmother, but is a powerful force in its own right ... An ally is like a half-broken horse, a horse with spirit. A horse that will carry you many days, only to suddenly knock you off on a low branch.

The fairy tale of Jack and the Beanstalk is symbolic of human endeavors that harness imagination in the service of dissatisfaction with objective reality, which itself is neither fixed nor monolithic. And yet dissatisfaction with one's life goes beyond the mundane to encompass finitude, the borders of space and time, loss, aging, and death. The vast technological edifice in which we are embedded and which continually breaks the bounds of what is objectively possible testifies to the necessity of fantasy in reshaping and even recreating reality. One might see every gain made by science, technology, and medicine as an exercise in wish fulfillment (Knafo & Lo Bosco, 2017).

Some artists who view their work itself in terms of addiction maintain that while serving certain healthy functions, the compulsive drive to create also has the potential to cause great suffering. Consider those who find themselves haunted by the isolation and painstaking emotional investment required to create inspired works (Cheever, 1990; Knafo, 2012). Consider, too, those who wish to improve their lives and find greater inner peace, yet are resistant to change for fear of losing their creative inspiration. For instance, if early development occurs in an environment in which omnipotent illusions and reality are conceived of as sharply separated and mutually exclusive, then the capacity to fashion such fantasies into adaptive and creative outlets may be jeopardized. If a person is not able to find a delicate balance between the two, they may suffer an addictive devotion to illusions resulting in either a removal from reality or despair in the face of it (Mitchell, 2000).

In the authors' view, the manifestations of omnipotent fantasies in creativity are not always healthy, and in many ways they are not so different from those occurring in compulsive drug use. Moreover, narcissistic illusions driving addictions as well as creativity often stem from early loss or traumatic experiences and may be maladaptive and constricting in nature. On the other hand, the theory that the narcissistic illusions of addictions are pathological does not consider the adaptive aspects that substances provide for many users. Ten Berge (1999) found that substances uncover buried – childlike – aspects of the mind and establish contact with deeper levels of the psyche. Freud described this effect during the period he used cocaine: "You perceive an increase of self-control and possess more vitality and capacity for work … Long intensive mental or physical work is performed without any fatigue" (Jones, 1953/1961, p. 82).

Using drugs or alcohol can also help some artists deal with specific anxieties that are aroused by the creative process itself. Sex, too, serves the function of coping with anxieties, fears, and trauma. The regressive pull that takes place during the primary phase of creativity brings with it a great deal of anxiety (Knafo, 2012). Such an encounter may be colored by primal fears that are frequently experienced in terms of life-or-death. Rothenberg (1990) found that a cognitive strain exists in artists and innovators because their thinking processes often defy the usual rules of logic and reason. Anxieties generated from the creative process may cripple some artists, who then use substances to bring them down to a level that permits the continuation of creative work. Sensitivity, shyness, insecurity, and isolation are bound to coexist in the lives of many, if not most, creative individuals. Creativity is a solitary occupation; time spent alone is needed to generate and implement ideas. Such requisite isolation offers an escape from the stress of social situations, but it also produces loneliness and requires the creative person to labor for extended periods of time with little or no emotional support from others. Compulsive acts and/or substances, like alcohol, are known to provide courage for those who lack it and companionship for those who seek it.

Studying the associations among omnipotent fantasies, creativity, and addiction highlights both the precious and the precarious states of being that humans inhabit and strive to sustain. The destruction of conventional reality is necessary for creativity, and substances or compulsive acts are employed in the service of this destruction. Yet the paradox of the infatuation with magic is that the tables eventually turn and the master becomes a slave, one left to succumb to the creativity-destroying and life-limiting processes of addiction. The best therapeutic solution to this paradox is to chart a course between the Scylla and Charybdis of grandiose fantasy and the demands of day-to-day quotidian life.

References

Alcoholic Anonymous World Services (1976). *Alcoholics anonymous* (3rd ed.). New York, NY: Alcoholic Anonymous World Services, Inc.

Almond, R. (1997). Omnipotence and power. In C. S. Ellman & J. Reppen (Eds.), *Omnipotent fantasies and the vulnerable self* (p. 11). Northvale, NJ: Aronson.

American Psychiatric Association (2013). *Diagnostic and statistical manual of mental disorders-5* (5th ed.). Washington, DC: American Psychiatric Association.

Andersen, C. P. (2012). *Mick: The wild life and mad genius of Jagger.* London: Robson Press.

Andreasen, N. (2005). *The creating brain: The neuroscience of genius.* New York, NY: Plume.

Andreason, N. C. (1987). Creativity and mental illness: Prevalence rates in writers and their first-degree relatives. *American Journal of Psychiatry*, 144(10), 1288–1292.

Andreason, N. C. & Glick, I. D. (1988). Bipolar affective disorder and creativity: Implications and clinical management. *Comprehensive Psychiatry, 29*(3), 207–217.

Aron, L. (1995). The internalized primal scene. *Psychoanalytic Dialogues: The International Journal of Relational Perspectives*, 5, 195–237.

Bach, S. (1994). *The language of perversion and the language of love.* Northvale, NJ: Aronson.

Bataille, G. (1957). *L'érotisme.* Paris, France: Minuit.

Baudelaire, C. (1864/1970). *Paris spleen* (M. Sorrell, Ed. & Trans.). Richmond, England: London House. Retrieved on July 29, 2017 from https://books.google.com/books?id=15craP5h4O4C&printsec=frontcover&source=gbs_g e_summary_r&cad=0#v=onepage&q&f=false

Baudelaire, C. (1974). Envirez-vous. *Yale French Studies*, 50, 5–7.

Baudelaire, C. (1982). *Les fleurs du mal* (R. Howard, Trans.). Boston. MA: Godine Publisher Inc.

Baudelaire, C. (1996). *Artificial paradises.* New York, NY: Citadel Press. (Original work published in 1859)

Beahm, G. (1989). *The Stephen King companion.* New York, NY: Andrews and McMeel.

Becker, E. (1973/1997). *The denial of death.* New York, NY: Simon & Schuster.

Biello, D. (2011, July 26). Is there a link between creativity and addiction? *Scientific American*, 20. Retrieved on July 29, 2017 from www.scientificamerican.com/article/is-there-a-link-between-creativity-and-addiction

Boler, K. (2004). *A drinking companion: Alcohol and the lives of writers.* New York, NY: Cardoza.

Bollas, C. (1987). *The shadow of the object: Psychoanalysis of the unthought known.* New York, NY: Columbia University Press.

Boon, M. (2002). *The road of excess: The history of writers on drugs.* Cambridge, MA: Harvard University Press.

Brand, R. (2008). *My booky wook: A memoir of sex, drugs and stand-up.* London: Hodder.

Bukowski, C. (1982). *Ham on rye.* New York, NY: Black Sparrow Books.

Bukowski, C. (1993/2003). *Run with the hunted: A Charles Bukowski reader.* New York, NY: Harper Perennial.

Burroughs, A. (2003). *Dry.* New York, NY: St. Martin's Press.

Callender, K. (2013). The Serenity Prayer by Reinhold Niebuhr. *Psych Central.* Retrieved on July 17, 2017, from https://blogs.psychcentral.com/lessons/2013/06/the-serenity-prayer

Centers for Disease Control and Prevention (2007). Increasing prevalence of parent-reported attention-deficit/hyperactivity disorder among children, *Morbidity and Mortality Weekly Report*, 59(44), pp. 1439–1443.

Chasseguet-Smirguel, J. (1983). Perversion and the universal law. *International Review of Psychoanalysis*, 10, 293–301.

Chasseguet-Smirguel, J. (1984). *Creativity and perversion.* New York, NY: Norton.

Cheever, J. (1990). *The journals of John Cheever.* New York, NY: Alfred A. Knopf.

Colburn, S. E. (1988). *Anne Sexton: Telling the tale.* Ann Arbor, MI: University of Michigan Press.

Coleridge, S.T. (1899). Kubla Khan. In T. F. Huntington (Ed.), *Coleridge's Ancient Mariner, Kubla Khan and Christabel* (pp. 35–37). New York, NY: The MacMillan Company.

Crowley, A. (1973/1991). *Magick without tears.* Las Vegas, NV: New Falcon Publications.

Currey, M. (2013). *Daily rituals: How artists work.* New York, NY: Knopf.

De Brosses, C., Morris, R., & Leonard, D. (2017). *The returns of fetishism: Charles de Brosses and the afterlives of an idea.* Chicago, IL: University of Chicago Press.

DeLong, G. R. (1990). Lithium treatment and bipolar disorders in childhood. *North Carolina Medical Journal*, 51, 152–154.

De Nicholas, A. T. (1998). *Meditations through the Rg Veda: Four dimensional man.* York Beach, ME: Weiser Books.

De Quincy, T. (1950). *Confessions of an English opium-eater.* New York, NY: Heritage Press. (Original work published 1821)

Derrida, J. (2003). The rhetoric of drugs. In A. Alexander, & M. Roberts (Eds.), *High culture: Reflections on addiction and modernity* (pp. 19–44). Albany: State University of NY Press.

Director, L. (2002). The value of relational psychoanalysis in the treatment of chronic drug and alcohol use. *Psychoanalytic Dialogues: The International Journal of Relational Perspectives*, 12(4), 551–580.

Director, L. (2005). Encounters with omnipotence in the psychoanalysis of substance users. *Psychoanalytic Dialogues: The International Journal of Relational Perspectives*, 15(4), 567–587.

Dixon, L., Kroopf, S., & Kavanaugh, R. (Producers) & Burger, N. (Director). (2011). *Limitless* [Motion picture]. Beverly Hills, CA: Relativity Media.

Dodes, L. (1990). Addiction, helplessness, and narcissistic rage. *Psychoanalytic Quarterly*, 59, 398–419.

Dodes, L. (2003). *The heart of addiction*. New York, NY: HarperCollins Publishers.

Dodes, L. (2011). New psychoanalytic understanding of addiction. *The American Psychoanalyst*, 45(3), 17.

Donald, D. H. (1987). *Look homeward: A life of Thomas Wolfe*. New York, NY: Ballantine Books.

Ehrenzweig, A. (1967). *The hidden order of art*. Berkeley, CA: University of California Press.

Eliot, T. S. (1963). *Collected poems 1909–1962*. London: Faber & Faber.

Ellison, M., Jonze, S., & Landay, V. (Producers), & Jonze, S. (Director). (2013). *Her* [Motion picture]. Los Angeles, CA: Annapurna Pictures.

Ellman, C. S. & Reppen, J. (Eds.). (1997). Introduction. In *Omnipotent fantasies and the vulnerable self* (pp. xiii–xv). Northvale, NJ: Jason Aronson.

Fairbairn, R. (1952). *Psychoanalytic studies of the personality*. New York, NY: Routledge.

Felstiner, M. L. (1994). *To paint her life: Charlotte Salomon in the Nazi era*. New York, NY: HarperCollins Publishers.

Fenichel, O. (1945/1996). *The psychoanalytic theory of neurosis*. New York, NY: W. W. Norton & Company.

Feuerstein, G. (2001). *The Yoga tradition: Its history, literature, philosophy, and practice*. Prescott, AZ: Hohm Press.

Fitch, N. R. (1993). *Anais: The erotic life of Anais Nin*. New York, NY: Little, Brown & Company.

Flora, S. R. (2004). *The power of reinforcement*. Albany, NY: SUNY Press.

Fraiberg, S. H. (1959). *The magic years*. New York, NY: Simon & Schuster, 2008.

Freud, S. (1950). Extracts from the Fliess papers, 1887–1902. In J. Strachey (Ed. & Trans.), *The standard edition of the complete psychological works of Sigmund Freud* (Vol. 1, pp. 173–280). London: Hogarth Press. (Original work published in 1897)

Freud, S. (1953). Three essays on the theory of sexuality. In J. Strachey (Ed. & Trans.), *The standard edition of the complete psychological works of Sigmund Freud* (Vol. 7, pp. 135–174). London: Hogarth Press. (Original work published in 1905)

Freud, S. (1955a). Beyond the pleasure principle. In J. Strachey (Ed. & Trans.), *The standard edition of the complete psychological works of Sigmund Freud* (Vol. 18, pp. 1–64). London: Hogarth Press. (Original work published in 1920)

Freud, S. (1955b). Creative writers and day-dreamers. In J. Strachey (Ed. & Trans.), *The standard edition of the complete psychological works of Sigmund Freud* (Vol. 9, pp. 142–156). London: Hogarth Press. (Original work published in 1909)

Freud, S. (1955c). Notes upon a case of obsessional neurosis. In J. Strachey (Ed. & Trans.), *The standard edition of the complete psychological works of Sigmund Freud* (Vol. 10, pp. 151–318). London: Hogarth Press. (Original work published in 1909)

Freud, S. (1957). Five lectures on psycho-analysis. In J. Strachey (Ed. & Trans.), *The standard edition of the complete psychological works of Sigmund Freud* (Vol. 11, pp. 7–55). London: Hogarth Press. (Original work published in 1910)

Freud, S. (1958a). Formulations on the two principles of mental functioning. In J. Strachey (Ed. & Trans.), *The standard edition of the complete psychological works of Sigmund Freud* (Vol. 12, pp. 213–226). London, England: Hogarth Press. (Original work published in 1911)

Freud, S. (1958b). On narcissism. In J. Strachey (Ed. & Trans.), *The standard edition of the complete psychological works of Sigmund Freud* (Vol. 14, pp. 67–102). London: Hogarth Press. (Original work published in 1914)

Freud, S. (1961b). The future of an illusion. In J. Strachey (Ed. & Trans.), *The standard edition of the complete psychological works of Sigmund Freud* (Vol. 21, pp. 21–43), London: Hogarth Press. (Original work published in 1927)

Freud, S. (1961c). Totem and taboo: Some points of agreement between the mental lives of savages and neurotics. In J. Strachey (Ed. & Trans.), *The standard edition of the complete psychological works of Sigmund Freud* (Vol. 13, pp. xii 2013;162). London: Hogarth Press. (Original work published in 1913)

Freud, S. (1961d). Civilization and its discontents. In J. Strachey (Ed. & Trans.), *The standard edition of the complete psychological works of Sigmund Freud* (Vol. 21, pp. 57–145). London: Hogarth Press. (Original work published in 1930)

Freud, S. (1986). The relation of the poet to day-dreaming. In B. Nelson (Ed.), *On creativity and the unconscious: The psychology of art, literature, love, and religion* (pp. 44–54). New York: Harper. (Original work published in 1908)

Fromm, E. (1956/2006). *The art of loving*. New York, NY: Harper & Row.

Generation Film (2013, November 20). *Her*: Spike Jonze's prophetic reflection on social isolation and dependency on evolving technologies is as sweet as it is disconcerting [Movie review]. Retrieved from https://generationfilm.net/2013/11/20/movie-review-her-spike-jonzes-prophetic-reflection-on-social-isolation-and-the-dependency-on-evolving-technologies-is-as-sweet-as-it-is-disconcerting

George, D. H. (1987). *Oedipus Anne: The poetry of Anne Sexton*. Champaign: University of Illinois Press. Retrieved from www.english.illinois.edu/maps/poets/s_z/sexton/career.htm

Ghent, E. (1999). Masochism, submission, surrender: Masochism as a perversion of surrender. In S. A. Mitchell and L. Aron (Eds.), *Relational psychoanalysis: The emergence of a tradition* (pp. 213–242). Hillsdale, NJ: The Analytic Press.

Goliszek, A. (2014, December 22). The stress-sex connection. *Psychology Today*. Retrieved from www.psychologytoday.com/us/blog/how-the-mind-heals-the-body/201412/the-stress-sex-connection

Goodwin, D. W. (1988). *Alcohol and the writer*. New York, NY: Andrews and McMeel.

Green, R., Stoller, R. J., & MacAndrew, C. (1966). Attitudes toward sex transformation procedures. *Archives of General Psychiatry*, 15, 178–182.

Greenacre, P. (1971). The childhood of the artist. In *Emotional growth* (Vol. 2, pp. 479–504). New York, NY: International Universities Press. (Original work published 1957)

Gustafson, R. & Källmén, H. (1989a). The effect of alcohol intoxication on primary and secondary processes in male social drinkers. *British Journal of Addiction*, 84, 1507–1513.

Gustafson, R. & Källmén, H. (1989b). Alcohol effects on cognitive personality style in women with special reference to primary and secondary process. *Alcoholism: Clinical and Experimental Research*, 13, 644–648.

Hajcak, F. C. (1976). The effects of alcohol on creativity (Doctoral dissertation). Ann Arbor, MI: UMI, Dissertation Services.

Harrison (2009). *Undying love: The true story of a passion that defied death*. New York, NY: St. Martin's Press.

Hart, S. (2011). *The impact of attachment*. New York, NY: W. W. Norton & Company.

Haworth, A. (2013). Why have young people in Japan stopped having sex? *The Guardian*. Retrieved from www.theguardian.com/world/2013/oct/20/young-people-japan-stopped-having-sex

Hedren, T. (2016). *Tippi: A memoir*. New York, NY: William Morrow.

Herzberg, J. (1981). *Charlotte: Life or theater: An autobiographical play by Charlotte Salomon*. (L. Venewitz, Trans.). New York, NY: Viking.

Hughes, S. M. (1991, December). The Sexton tapes. *The Pennsylvania Gazette*, 90(3), 20–28. Retrieved from www.psych.upenn.edu/history/orne/hughessextontapes.html

Iacono, A. M. (2016). *The history and theory of fetishism* (V. Tchernichova & M. Boria, Trans). New York, NY: Palgrave Macmillan.

Isaacs, S. (1948). The nature and function of phantasy. *The International Journal of Psychoanalysis*, 29, 73–97.

Jamison, K. R. (1989). Mood disorders and patterns of creativity in British writers and artists. *Psychiatry*, 52, 125–134.

Jamison, K. R. (1993). *Touched by fire: Manic-depressive illness and the artistic temperament*. New York, NY: Free Press.

Jones, E. (1953/1961). *The life and work of Sigmund Freud: Vol. 3. The last phase 1919–1939*. Oxford: Basic Books.

Jung, C. G. (1952). Psychology and literature. In B. Ghiselin (Ed.), *The creative process*. New York, NY: New American Library.

Kalin, R., McClelland, D. C., & Kahn, M. (1965). The effects of male social drinking on fantasy. *Journal of Personality and Social Psychology*, 1, 441–452.

Karr, M. (2009). *Lit: A memoir*. New York, NY: Harper.

Kazin, A. (1976). "The giant killer": Drink and the American writer. *Commentary*, 61, 44–50.

Kenton, S. (1960). The Playboy panel: Narcotics and the jazz musicians. *Playboy*, 7 (11), 35–48, 117–118, 126–127.

Kernberg, O. (1975). *Borderline conditions and pathological narcissism*. New York, NY: Jason Aronson.

Kernberg, O. (1986). Factors in the psychoanalytic treatment of narcissistic personality disorders. In A. P. Morrison (Ed.), *Essential papers on narcissism*. New York, NY: New York University Press.

Khantzian, E. (1995). Self-regulation vulnerabilities in substance abusers: Treatment implications. In S. Dowling (Ed.), *The psychology and treatment of addictive behavior* (pp. 65–100). Madison, CT: International Universities Press.

Khantzian, E. (1999). *Treating addiction as a human process*. Lanham, MD: Jason Aronson.

King, S. (1981). *Danse macabre*. New York, NY: Gallery Books.

King, S. (1977). *The shining*. New York, NY: Penguin Group.

King, S. (1997). *60 Minutes* interview. February 16, 1997.

King, S. (2000). *On writing: A memoir of the craft*. New York, NY: Scribner.

King, S. (2013). Good reads: Stephen King quotes. Retrieved from www.goodreads.com/quotes/76139-books-are-a-uniquely-portable-magic

Kirby, T. (1999). Hitch: Alfred the great [Television series episode]. In T. Kirby (Producer) & T. Kirby (Director), *Reputations*. London: British Broadcasting Company.

Klein, M. (1929/2002). Personification in the play of children. International Journal of Psychoanalysis, 10, 193–204.

Klein, M. (1940/1988). Mourning and its relation to manic-depressive states. *International Journal of Psycho-Analysis*, 21, 125–153.

Klein, M. (1955). The psychoanalytic play technique. *American Journal of Orthopsychiatry*, 25, 223–237.

Klibansky, R., Panofsky, E., & Saxl, F. (1964). *Saturn and melancholy: Studies in the history of natural philosophy*. Nashville, TN: Thomas Nelson & Sons.

Knafo, D. (2008). The senses grow skilled in their craving: Thoughts on creativity and addiction. *Psychoanalytic Review*, 95(4), 571–700.

Knafo, D. (2009). *In her own image: Women's self-representation in twentieth-century art*. Madison, NJ: Fairleigh Dickinson University Press.

Knafo, D. (2010). *The sexual illusionist*. Unpublished manuscript.

Knafo, D. (2012). *Dancing with the unconscious: The art of psychoanalysis and the psychoanalysis of art*. New York, NY: Taylor & Francis.

Knafo, D. & Lo Bosco, R. (2017). *The age of perversion: Desire and technology in psychoanalysis and culture*. London: Routledge.

Knapp, C. (1996). *Drinking: A love story*. New York, NY: Bantam Doubleday Dell Publishing Group.

Kohut, H. (1966/2011). Forms and transformations of narcissism. In P. H. Ornstein (Ed.), *The search for the self: Selected writings of Heinz Kohut: 1950–1978* (Kindle edition, Chapter 32, Section 2, para. 9). London: Karnac Books.

Kohut, H. (1971/2011). *The analysis of the self*. New York, NY: International Universities Press, 2000.

Kohut, H. (1977/2009a). Preface. In J. I. Blaine & D. A. Julius (Eds.), *Psychodynamics of drug dependence*. Rockville, MD: National Institute on Drug Abuse.

Kohut, H. (1977/2009b). *The restoration of the self*. Chicago, IL: University of Chicago Press.

Koob, G. (2011). An interview with George Koob. *Close to Home: Moyers on Addiction*. Retrieved from www.thirteen.org/closetohome/science/html/koob.html

Koski-Jännes, A. (1985). Alcohol and literary creativity – The Finnish experience. *Journal of Creative Behavior*, 19, 120–136.

Kraeplin, E. (1921/2002). *Manic-depressive insanity and paranoia*. London: Thoemmes Press.

Kramer-Richards, A. (2003). A fresh look at perversion. *Journal of the American Planning Association*, 51(4), 1199–1218.

Kris, E. (1952). *Psychoanalytic explorations in art*. New York, NY: International Universities Press.

Kristeva, J. (1982). *Powers of horror: An essay on abjection* (L. S. Roudiez, Trans.). New York, NY: Columbia University Press.

Krystal, H. (1982). Alexithymia and the effectiveness of psychoanalytic treatment. *International Journal of Psychoanalytic Psychotherapy*, 9, 353–388.

Krystal, H. (1995). Disorders of emotional development in addictive behavior. In S. Dowling (Ed.), *The psychology and treatment of addictive behavior* (pp. 65–100). Madison, CT: International Universities Press.

Lah, K. (2009, December 17). Tokyo man marries game character. *CNN*. Retrieved from www.cnn.com/2009/WORLD/asiapcf/12/16/japan.virtual.wedding

Lange, A. & Bozza, A. (2008). *Too fat to fish*. New York, NY: Spiegel & Grau.

Levertov, D. (1981). *Light up the cave*. New York, NY: New Directions.

Ludwig, A. M. (1994). Mental illness and creative activity in female writers. *American Journal of Psychiatry*, 151 (11), 1650–1656.

Lyng, S. (1990). Edgework: A social psychological analysis of voluntary risk taking. *American Journal of Sociology*, 95(4), 851–886.

Macdonald, A. & Reich, A. (Producers), & Garland, A. (Director). (2015). *Ex machina* [Motion picture]. London: Universal Pictures International.

Markow, D. & McCormick, J. (Producers), & Dullaghan, J. (Director). (2003). *Born into this*. [Motion picture]. New York, NY: Magnolia Pictures.

Marlowe, A. (1999). *How to stop time: Heroin from A to Z*. New York, NY: Basic Books.

Marnham, P. (1992). *The man who wasn't Maigret: Portrait of Georges Simenon*. London: Bloomsbury Publishing.

Mastro, S. & Zimmer-Gembeck, M. J. (2015). Let's talk openly about sex: Sexual communication, self-esteem and efficacy as correlates of sexual well- being. *European Journal of Developmental Psychology*, 12(5), 579–598. doi: doi:10.1080/17405629.2015.1054373

McDougall, J. (1972). Primal scene and sexual perversion. *The International Journal of Psycho-Analysis*, 53, 371–384.

Mehlman, P. (2005, November 15). Zuckerman juiced. *The New York Times*. Retrieved from www.nytimes.com/2005/11/14/opinion/zuckerman-juiced.html

Middlebrook, D. W. (1991). *Anne Sexton: A biography*. Boston, MA: Houghton Mifflin Company.

Mitchell, S. A. (1988). *Relational concepts in psychoanalysis: An integration*. Cambridge, MA: Harvard University Press.

Mitchell, S. A. (2000). *Relationality: From attachment to intersubjectivity*. Hillsdale, NJ: The Analytic Press, Inc.

Mitchell, S. A. (2002). *Can love last? The fate of romance over time*. New York, NY: W. W. Norton & Company.

Morin (1995). *The erotic mind: Unlocking the inner sources of sexual passion and fulfillment*. New York, NY: HarperPerennial Publishers.

Nin, A. & Stuhlman, G. (Ed.). (1969). *The diary of Anais Nin: Volume Three 1939–1944*. Orlando, FL: Harcourt Brace Jovanovich Publishers.

NIDA Notes (2014, December). 2003 survey reveals increase in prescription drug abuse, sharp drop in abuse of hallucinogens. *NIDA Notes*, 19(4), 14.

Nietzsche, F. (1870/2013). The Dionysian worldview. In I. Allen & F. Ulfers (Trans.), *The Dionysian vision of the world* (pp. 29–58). Minneapolis, MN: University of Minnesota Press.

Nietzsche, F. (1872/1956). The birth of tragedy. In F. Golffing (Trans.), *The birth of tragedy and genealogy of morals*. New York, NY: Doubleday Anchor.

Nin, A. & Stuhlmann, G. (Ed.). (1966). *The diary of Anais Nin: Volume Three 1931–1934*. New York, NY: Harcourt, Brace & World.

Norlander, T. (1999). Inebriation and inspiration? A review of the research on alcohol and creativity. *Journal of Creative Behavior*, 33 (1), 22–44.

Norman, P. (2012). *Mick Jagger*. New York, NY: Harper Collins Publishers.

Norden, E. (1983, June). The Playboy interview: Stephen King. *Playboy Magazine*.

Novick, J. & Novick, K. K. (2001). Two systems of self-regulation. *Psychoanalytic Social Work Journal*, 8, 95–122.

Novick, K. K. & Novick, J. (2003). Two systems of self-regulation and the differential application of psychoanalytic technique. *The American Journal of Psychoanalysis,* 63, 1–20.

Odier, D. (1970). *The job: Interviews with William Burroughs.* New York, NY: Jonathan Cape.

Ogden, T. H. (1995). Analysing forms of aliveness and deadness of the transference-countertransference. *The International Journal of Psycho-Analysis,* 76, 695–709.

Oxford University Press. (2009). *The Oxford Pocket Dictionary of Current English.* New York, NY: Oxford University Press.

Paglia, C. (1990). *Sexual personae: Art and decadence from Nefertiti to Emily Dickinson.* New York, NY: Vintage Books.

Pendell, D. (1995). *Pharmako/poeia: Plant powers, poisons, and herbcraft.* Berkeley, CA: North Atlantic Books.

Perel, E. (2006). *Mating in captivity: Reconciling the erotic and the domestic.* New York, NY: HarperCollins.

Phillips, A. (1998). *A defense of masochism.* New York, NY: St. Martin's Press.

Phillpotts, E. (1918). *A shadow passes.* London: Cecil Palmer and Hayward.

Plant, S. (1999). *Writing on drugs.* New York, NY: Farrar, Straus, & Giroux.

Plath, S. (1963/2016). *The bell jar.* New York, NY: HarperCollins Publishers.

Platt, C. (1983). *Dream makers, Volume II.* New York, NY: Berkley Books.

Pressman, M. (2011, April 5). Q&A: John Richardson on Picasso's "uncontrollable" sex drive. *Vanity Fair.* Retrieved from www.vanityfair.com/culture/2011/04/qa-john-richardson-on-picassos-uncontrollable-sex-drive

Rank, O. (1932/1989). *Art and the artist: Creative urge and personality development.* New York, NY: Norton.

Rank, O. (1929/1978). *Truth and reality* (J. Taft, Trans.). New York, NY: Norton.

Reid, J. A., Haskell, R. A., Dillahunt-Aspillaga, C., & Thor, J. A. (2013). Contemporary review of empirical and clinical studies of trauma bonding in violent or exploitative relationships. *International Journal of Psychology Research,* 8(1), 37–73.

Richards, R. L., Kinney, D. K., Lunde, I., & Benet, M. (1988). Creativity in manic-depressives, cyclothymes, and their normal first-degree relatives: A preliminary report. *Journal of Abnormal Psychology,* 97, 281–288.

Richman, S. (2014). *Mended by the muse: Creative transformations of trauma.* London: Routledge.

Rogak, L. (2008). *Haunted heart: The life and times of Stephen King.* New York, NY: Thomas Dunne Books.

Rothenberg, A. (1990). *Creativity & madness: New findings and old stereotypes.* Baltimore, MD: John Hopkins University Press.

Santora, P. B., Dowell, M. L., & Henningfield, J. E. (2010). *Addiction and art.* Baltimore, MD: Johns Hopkins University Press.

Salvio, P. M. (2007). *Anne Sexton: Teacher of weird abundance.* Albany: SUNY Press.

Scheff, D. (2008). *Beautiful boy.* Boston, MA:Houghton Mifflin Harcourt.

Schildkraut, J. J., Hirshfeld, A. J., & Murphy, J. M. (1994). Mind and mood in modern art, II: Depressive disorders, spirituality, and early deaths in the abstract expressionist artists of the New York School. *The American Journal of Psychiatry,* 151(4), 482–489.

Schjeldahl, P. (2001, July 9). Picasso's lust: Was sex the artist's real muse? *The New Yorker.* Retrieved from www.newyorker.com/magazine/2001/07/09/picassos-lust

Schore, A. (1994). *Affect regulation and the origin of the self: The neurobiology of emotional development*. Mahwah, NJ: Erlbaum.

Segal, H. (1974). Delusion and artistic creativity: Some reflections on reading "The Spire" by William Golding. *International Review of Psycho-Analysis*, 1, 135–142.

Segal, H. (1991). Art and the depressive position. In *Dream, phantasy and art* (pp. 85–100). London: Tavistock and Routledge.

Seinfeld, J. (1991). *The empty core: An object relations approach to psychotherapy of the schizoid personality*. Northvale, NJ: Jason Aronson.

Seligman, M. E. P. (1998). The prediction and prevention of depression. In M. E. P. Seligman (Ed.), *The science of clinical psychology: Accomplishments and future directions* (pp. 201–214). Washington, DC: American Psychological Association.

Sexton, A. (1978). Letters to Dr. Y. In L. G. Sexton (Ed.), *Words for Dr. Y: Uncollected poems and three stories*. Boston, MA: Houghton Mifflin Company.

Sexton, A. (1985a). Interview with Barbara Kevles. In S. E. Colburn (Ed.), *No evil star: Selected essays, interviews, and prose* (pp. 83–111). Ann Arbor, MI: University of Michigan Press. (Original work published in 1974)

Sexton, A. (1985b). Interview with Brigitte Weeks. In S. E. Colburn (Ed.), *No evil star: Selected essays, interviews, and prose* (pp. 112–118). Ann Arbor, MI: University of Michigan Press. (Original work published in 1968)

Sexton, A. (1985c). Interview with Harry Moore. In S. E. Colburn (Ed.), *No evil star: Selected essays, interviews, and prose* (pp. 41–69). Ann Arbor, MI: University of Michigan Press. (Original work published in 1968)

Sexton, A. (1985d). Interview with Patricia Marx. In S. E. Colburn (Ed.), *No evil star: Selected essays, interviews, and prose* (pp. 70–82). Ann Arbor, MI: University of Michigan Press. (Original work published in 1966)

Sexton, A. (1985e). The freak show. In S. E. Colburn (Ed.), *No evil star: Selected essays, interviews, and prose* (pp. 33–38). Ann Arbor, MI: University of Michigan Press. (Original work published in 1973)

Sexton, A. (1999a). Cripples and other stories. In *The complete poems of Anne Sexton* (pp. 160–163). Boston, MA: Mariner Books. (Original work published in 1965)

Sexton, A. (1999b). For John, who begs me not to enquire further. In *The complete poems of Anne Sexton* (pp. 34–35). Boston, MA: Mariner Books. (Original worked published in 1960)

Sexton, A. (1999c). Frenzy. In *The complete poems of Anne Sexton* (pp. 466–467). Boston MA: Mariner Books. (Original work published in 1975)

Sexton, A. (1999d). Killing the love. In *The complete poems of Anne Sexton* (pp. 529–530). Boston, MA: Mariner Books. (Original work published in 1976)

Sexton, A. (1999e). Live. In *The complete poems of Anne Sexton* (pp. 166–170). Boston, MA: Mariner Books. (Original work published in 1966)

Sexton, A. (1999f). The addict. In *The complete poems of Anne Sexton* (pp. 165–166). Boston, MA: Mariner Books. (Original work published in 1966)

Sexton, A. (1999g). The ambition bird. In *The complete poems of Anne Sexton* (pp. 299–300). Boston, MA:Mariner Books. (Original work published in 1972)

Sexton, A. (1999h). The civil war. In *The complete poems of Anne Sexton* (pp. 463–464). Boston, MA: Mariner Books. (Original work published in 1975)

Sexton, A. (1999i). The poet of ignorance. In *The complete poems of Anne Sexton* (pp. 433–434). Boston, MA: Mariner Books. (Original work published in 1975)

Sexton, A. (1999j). The rowing. In *The complete poems of Anne Sexton* (pp. 417–418). Boston, MA: Mariner Books. (Original work published in 1975)

Sexton, A. (1999k). The silence. In *The complete poems of Anne Sexton* (pp. 318–319). Boston, MA: Mariner Books. (Original work published in 1972)

Sexton, A. (1999l). Wanting to die. In *The complete poems of Anne Sexton* (pp. 142–143). Boston, MA: Mariner Books. (Original work published in 1964)

Sexton, A. (1999m). Words. In *The complete poems of Anne Sexton* (pp. 463–464). Boston, MA: Mariner Books. (Original work published in 1975)

Sexton, L. G. & Ames, L. (1977). *Anne Sexton: A self-portrait in letters.* Boston, MA: Houghton Mifflin Company.

Shabad, P. (2010). Everyone must get a turn: From omnipotence to respect for otherness: Reply to commentary. *Psychoanalytic Dialogues: The International Journal of Relational Perspectives, 20*(6), 733–737.

Shields, D. & Morrow, B. (2011). *The inevitable: Contemporary writers confront death.* New York, NY: W. W. Norton.

Skinner, B. F. (1976). *About behaviorism.* New York, NY: Vintage Books.

Skorczewski, D. M. (2012). *An accident of hope: The therapy tapes of Anne Sexton.* New York, NY: Taylor & Francis.

Slochower, J. A. (1998). Illusion and uncertainty in psychoanalytic writing. *International Journal of Psycho-Analysis, 79,* 333–347.

Smith, D. L. (1986). Omnipotence. *British Journal of Psychotherapy, 3,* 52–59.

Smith, T. (2008, June 6). Rowling's Harvard speech doesn't entrance all. *NPR.* Retrieved from www.npr.org/templates/story/story.php?storyId=91232541

Solms, M. & Turnbull, O. (2010). *The brain and the inner world: An introduction to the neuroscience of subjective experience.* New York, NY: Other Press.

Spignesi, S. J. (1991). *The complete Stephen King encyclopedia: The definitive guide to works of America's master of horror.* Chicago, IL: Contemporary Books.

Spoto, D. (1983). *The dark side of genius: The life of Alfred Hitchcock.* Boston, MA: Little, Brown & Company.

Stein, R. (2005). Why perversion? "False love" and the perverse pact. *International Journal of Psychoanalysis, 86*(3), 775–799.

Stevenson, R. L. (1909). *The strange case of Dr. Jekyll and Mr. Hyde.* New York, NY: Current Literature Publishing Company.

Stiles, K. (1992). Survival ethos and destruction art. *Discourse: Journal for Theoretical Studies in Media and Culture, 14,* 74–102.

Stoller, R. (1974). Hostility and mystery in perversion. *International Journal of Psychoanalysis, 55,* 426–434.

Stoller, R. (1975). *Perversion: The erotic form of hatred.* London: Karnac.

Storr, A. (1976). *The dynamics of creation.* Harmondsworth, England: Penguin Books.

Styron, W. (1990). *Darkness visible: A memoir of madness.* New York, NY: Vintage Books.

Tatarsky, A. (2002). *Harm reduction psychotherapy: A new treatment for drug and alcohol problems.* Lanham, MD: Rowman & Littlefield Publishers.

Ten Berge, J. (1999). Breakdown or breakthrough? A history of European research into drugs and creativity. *Journal of Creative Behavior, 33,* 257–276.

Ulman, R. B. & Paul, H. (2006). *The self-psychology of addiction and its treatment: Narcissus in wonderland.* New York, NY: Routledge.

Underwood, T. & Miller, C. (1988). *Bare bones: A conversation on terror with Stephen King*. New York, NY: McGraw-Hill.

Unger, R. M. (2007). *The self awakened: Pragmatism unbound*. Cambridge, MA: Harvard University Press.

Wall, G. (2001). *Flaubert: A life*. New York, NY: Farrar, Straus & Giroux.

Wanamaker, M. C. (1999). William Styron and the literature of early maternal loss. *Psychoanalytic Review*, 86, 403–432.

Weiss, A. (2003). Baudelaire, Artaud and the aesthetics of intoxication. In A. Alexander & M. Roberts (Eds.), *High culture: Reflections on addiction and modernity* (pp. 157–172). Albany, NY: State University of NY Press.

Welldon, E. (2009). Dancing with death. *British Journal of Psychotherapy*, 25(2), 149–182.

Welldon, E. (2011). *Playing with dynamite: A personal approach to the psychoanalytic understanding of perversions, violence, and criminality*. London: Karnac.

Wennersten, R. (1975, January). Paying for horses. *London Magazine*, 1(15), 35–54.

Whitman, S. H. (1922). *Edgar Poe and his critics*. New York, NY: Rudd & Carleton.

Winnicott, D. W. (1945). Primitive emotional development. *International Journal of Psychoanalysis*, 26, 137–143.

Winnicott, D. W. (1949). Hate in the counter-transference. *International Journal of Psycho-Analysis*, 30, 69–74.

Winnicott, D. W. (1971). *Playing and reality*. New York, NY: Routledge Classics.

Winter, D. (1984). *Stephen King: The art of darkness*. New York, NY: New American Library Books.

Wisman, A. & Goldenberg, J. L. (2005). From the grave to the cradle: Evidence that mortality salience engenders a desire for offspring. *Journal of Personality and Social Psychology*, 89(1), 46–61.

Wood, P. B., Gove, W. R., Wilson, J. A., & Cochran, J. K. (1997). Nonsocial reinforcement and habitual criminal conduct: An extension of learning theory. *Criminology*, 35, 335–366.

Wurmser, L. (1978/1995). *The hidden dimension: The psychodynamics of compulsive drug use*. Northvale, NJ: Jason Aronson.

Wurmser, L. (1979). Idealization and aggression in Beethoven's creativity. *American Imago*, 36, 328–344.

Wurmser, L. (2000). *The power of the inner judge*. New York, NY: Jason Aronson.

Yanes, A. (2014, April 18). Just say yes? The rise of "study drugs" in college. CNN. Retrieved from www.cnn.com/2014/04/17/health/adderall-college-students/index.html

Zuvekas, S. H., Vitiello, B., & Norquist, G. S. (2012). Stimulant medication use in children: a 12-year perspective. *American Journal of Psychiatry*, 169(2), 160–166.

Index

For Product Safety Concerns and Information please contact our EU
representative GPSR@taylorandfrancis.com
Taylor & Francis Verlag GmbH, Kaufingerstraße 24, 80331 München, Germany

www.ingramcontent.com/pod-product-compliance
Lightning Source LLC
Chambersburg PA
CBHW070345270326
41926CB00017B/4003

9 781138 956094